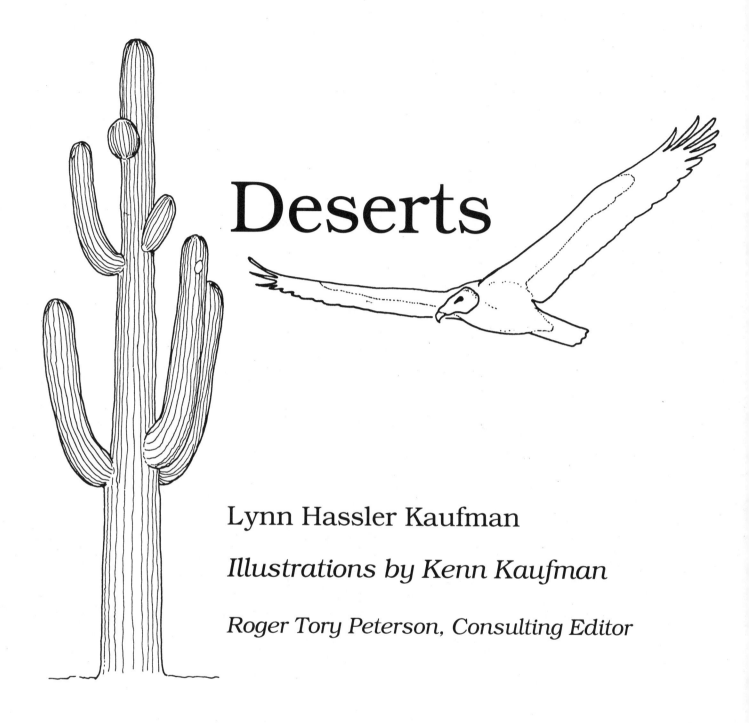

Deserts

Lynn Hassler Kaufman

Illustrations by Kenn Kaufman

Roger Tory Peterson, Consulting Editor

*Sponsored by
the National Wildlife Federation
and the National Audubon Society*

Houghton Mifflin Company Boston New York 1993

For permission to reproduce selections
from this book, write to Permissions,
Houghton Mifflin Company,
215 Park Avenue South,
New York, New York 10003.

Printed in the United States of America

HES 10 9 8 7 6 5 4 3 2 1

Introduction

A quick eye, trained to see details, is required for exploring the outdoors. The shape of a cactus, the color of a bird's wing, or the pattern on a lizard's skin are details that distinguish these species from other similar ones. To help them identify plants and animals, most beginning naturalists soon learn to use Field Guides, such as the Field Guide to Birds. These handy, pocket-size books offer shortcuts to identification, with clear illustrations complete with arrows pointing to the special features of each species.

This coloring book is a field guide for those who want to sharpen their powers of observation. By filling in the illustrations, you will condition your memory for the time you spend outdoors identifying animals and plants. You will learn to recognize the surprisingly diverse colors of the desert.

Exploring nature can be a game, a sport, an art, or a science. Whatever you make of it, spending time outdoors will sharpen your senses, especially your eyes. If you draw or paint, you transfer the images of your eyes and mind onto paper. In the process, you become more aware of the natural world — the real world — and inevitably you become an environmentalist.

Since there are deserts in only a limited region of our country, many of us must make a special trip to visit a desert if we want to see a Gila Monster or a Greater Roadrunner in its native habitat. But as environmentalists, we still care deeply about these and all the planet's species, and we work to keep their habitats intact.

Most of you will find colored pencils best suited for coloring this book, but if you are handy with brushes and paints, you may prefer to fill in the outlines with watercolors. Crayons, too, can be used. Don't labor too much over getting the colors just right; have fun discovering the desert. That is the purpose of this coloring book.

Roger Tory Peterson

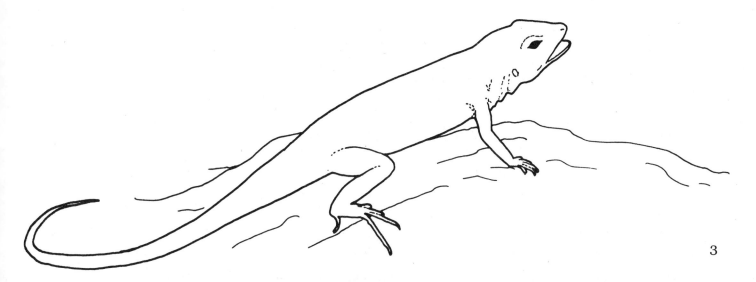

About This Book

What comes to mind when you hear the word desert? Do you think of a blazing sun beating down on a sea of sand, with the only plants a few cacti and the only sign of animal life a sun-bleached skull?

Many people think of deserts as empty, lifeless wastelands. But while this is true of some desert regions around the world, most deserts, including the ones found in North America, are unique natural habitats with their own fascinating array of plants and animals, from hummingbirds and hawks to cacti that grow as big as trees. Each of these species has adapted in special ways to the challenges of living in the desert. In smaller, specialized habitats within the desert, such as canyons and oases and along rivers, some plants and animals survive that could not make it elsewhere in the desert.

This book will introduce you to many of these plants and animals and explain how they live in the desert. Beside the name of each plant or animal you will find a number. The numbers match the color illustrations at the front and back of the book, which will show you the real-life colors of these species. Of course, colors vary in nature. The lizard you find in the desert might not look exactly like the one in the picture.

What is a Desert?

Some people define a desert as an area that receives less than 10 inches of rain per year. More important than the actual amount of rainfall, however, is how fast the water dries up — that is, how fast moisture evaporates. In a true desert, the rate of evaporation is greater than the rate of rainfall. Water evaporates faster in the high temperatures, low humidity, and drying winds found in our deserts.

Every Desert is Different

This coloring book will introduce you to the four deserts of North America: the Chihuahuan (chee-WAH-wahn), Great Basin, Mojave (moh-HAH-vay), and Sonoran. These deserts have no precise boundaries. But each desert has its own characteristics, including temperature, elevation, amount and timing of rain, soil types, and general terrain. These features determine what kind of plants grow in each region. The plant life, in turn, determines the animal life.

Chihuahuan Desert. This desert covers parts of southern New Mexico, southeastern Arizona, and west Texas and extends into Mexico. It has cold winters and hot summers. Rain falls mainly in summer, although the northwestern part gets some winter rain. The average annual rainfall is 6 to 12 inches. Elevation is mostly above 3,500 feet. There are few trees; most plants are shrubs, cacti, and annuals (plants that live for only one growing season).

Great Basin Desert. The Great Basin is the largest of the four North American deserts. It covers much of Nevada and Utah and parts of Washington, Oregon, California, Idaho, Colorado, Wyoming, New Mexico, and Arizona. This is also the desert with the highest elevation — most of it is above 4,000 feet. The Great Basin is known as a "cold desert" because winters are very cold, and it gets some winter snow. About 4 to 11 inches of rain and snow fall per year. The growing season for plants is short. Low-growing shrubs are the most common plants. There are few annuals, trees, or cacti.

Mojave Desert. The Mojave Desert is centered in southern California and stretches into Nevada, Utah, and Arizona. This is the smallest and driest of the four deserts. Only about 2 to 10 inches of rain falls in a year, most of it in winter, though the eastern section receives some summer rain. Elevation ranges from 2,000 to 4,000 feet. Winters are cool here, and summers are quite hot. Many kinds of low shrubs and annuals grow in the Mojave, as well as some cacti, but there are few trees.

Sonoran Desert. This desert covers southern Arizona, southeastern California, the lowlands of Baja California, and part of Sonora, Mexico. Elevation is mostly below 2,000 feet. Winter temperatures are usually mild, and summers are very hot. Most parts of this desert receive rains in both winter and summer, which allows for a greater variety of plant and animal species. Typical plants include tall cacti and other plants that can store water. Unlike the other deserts, the Sonoran has many trees, most of them fairly small.

Living in the Desert

Living in the desert presents some obvious challenges. Here are the biggest ones:

Lack of water. Since there is little rain, the species here must take advantage of water when it is available, and they must hold onto the moisture they have.

Extreme temperatures. Plants and animals that live in the desert must be able to stand both very high and very low temperatures. Wintertime temperatures often drop below freezing, and summertime temperatures can soar. The burning sun can be especially intense because there is little moisture in the air.

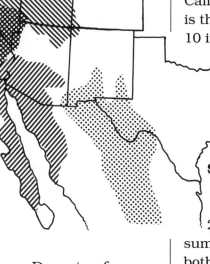

Deserts of
North America

Strong winds. Wind dries out the air and makes water evaporate faster. Winds can also cause dust and sand storms.

No place to hide. For animals, hiding places from predators are limited because the vegetation is often sparse. Many species rely on camouflage to survive.

The plants and animals that make their homes in the desert have adapted to these challenges in many different ways. Many species use a number of different strategies.

Strategies for Staying Alive

Many desert plants, such as the cacti, have tissue that expands to store water. These plants are called succulents. Some plants have very long roots that reach deep down to get underground water. Some have shallow spreading roots that are close to the surface of the soil so they can soak up as much water as possible when it does rain. Many have very small leaves; the smaller the leaf surface, the less moisture is lost to the air. Other plants have leathery leaves or leaves with waxy coatings, which help seal in the moisture. Some plants drop all their leaves during very dry weather to reduce water loss. The gray-green color so common to many desert plants helps to reflect sunlight. Spines, thorns, and hairs help protect some plants from being eaten by hungry creatures.

Animals have a distinct advantage over plants: they can move. This may mean moving only 10 feet to a small patch of shade under a sagebrush. It may mean moving under a rock that provides shade and insulation from the heat. For many desert animals, it means escaping into an underground burrow where the air is cooler and more humid.

Animals have many other ways of beating the heat. On a hot summer day, an antelope squirrel may lie spread out in the shade, flattening its belly against a patch of cool soil. Some lizards will also wriggle their bellies into the sand just under the surface, where it is slightly cooler.

Many animals rest or hide during the heat of the day and come out only at night. These are called nocturnal animals. The temperature is lower and the humidity is higher at night, making it a more comfortable time to search for food. Some animals are active at different times of day depending on the season. In the winter, they may be active at noon. As temperatures rise in spring, they may come out only in early morning and late afternoon. In the extreme heat of summer, they may search for food at dawn, dusk, and into the night.

Winter in the desert poses different problems. During the winter, many animals hibernate. In this inactive state they can survive a time of year when food is scarce and when the low temperature keeps their bodies from functioning normally. Snakes and most lizards hibernate, as do some mammals. Few birds hibernate, but some may migrate or leave the area in winter. On a cold winter day, the roadrunner will raise the feathers on its back, exposing its dark skin to the sun for a few minutes. The dark surface quickly absorbs the heat.

Desert animals also have special physical features to help them survive. Reptiles are covered with tough outer scales that prevent moisture loss. Kangaroo rats have specialized kidneys that allow them to go without drinking water. Spadefoot toads sleep buried in the ground for much of the year, waiting for rain, which they absorb directly through their skin.

Some physical adaptations are useful for protecting eyes and ears from blowing dust and sand. Kit foxes have heavy hairs on the insides of their ears to guard against blowing sand. Fringe-toed lizards have overlapping flaps of skin on their ears to keep sand grains out. Snakes cannot close their eyes because they have no eyelids, but their eyes are protected by hard, glassy scales.

In the wide-open desert, protective colors may be the only way to hide from predators. That's why so many desert animals are colored in earthy shades of brown and gray. Behavior can also be good camouflage. Some ground squirrels freeze and cling to the ground when threatened, and their sandy color perfectly matches the desert soil. Horned lizards also flatten themselves against the ground, becoming practically invisible.

Camouflage also applies to desert plants. The Night-blooming Cereus is a camouflage specialist. Most of the time, it looks like a bunch of dead sticks, making it unappealing to animals looking for a juicy plant to eat.

If You Visit a Desert

Deserts, along with the grassland and scrub that border them, cover almost a third of the Earth's land area. Although the deserts of North America are small compared to the Sahara or to some of the deserts in Asia or Australia, they hold an incredible variety of life forms. Nowhere else in the world is such an array of different types of desert so accessible to the traveler.

Perhaps you will travel through the desert one day. If you do, remember to take plenty of water and clothing to protect you from the sun, especially a hat with a wide brim. As you walk, see how many of the plants and animals from this book you recognize. Use all of your senses to experience this fascinating habitat. Smell the Creosote Bush after a rain. Carefully touch the spines on a cactus. Watch the glowing colors of the sky at sunset. And listen to the howl of the coyote as the moon rises over the desert.

The Chihuahuan Desert

Between the high plains of Texas and the cactus gardens of Arizona lies the dry region known as the Chihuahuan Desert. Imagine the impact this arid land must have had on the early pioneers, who traveled through the region more than a century ago. Although the area was new to them, Spanish explorers had been in the region for many years. This is why many of the plants and animals have Spanish names.

One of the most distinctive plants of the Chihuahuan Desert is the **Lechuguilla Agave (1)** (lay-choo-GHEE-yah ah-GAH-vee). Lechuguilla means "little lettuce" in Spanish. This plant has succulent, evergreen leaves and a single flower stalk 6 to 13 feet tall. The flowers are greenish white. Like other agaves, the Lechuguilla can live many years, but it blooms only once, and then the plant dies.

The **Chihuahuan Raven (2)** looks like a crow but has a heavier bill and a wedge-shaped tail. Also called White-necked Raven, its neck feathers have white bases visible only when its feathers are ruffled. It often searches for food in flocks. It eats mostly insects, dead animals, and bird eggs.

Lucky travelers in the Southwest may see a large, brown-streaked bird dashing across the road. A member of the cuckoo family, the **Greater Roadrunner (3)** can fly but prefers to run. It spends most of its time on the ground. When it is alarmed, it raises its shaggy crest, makes a clattering noise with its bill, and dashes off. Roadrunners prey on insects, frogs, rodents, birds, lizards, and snakes and

2. Chihuahuan Raven

3. Greater Roadrunner

1. Lechuguilla Agave

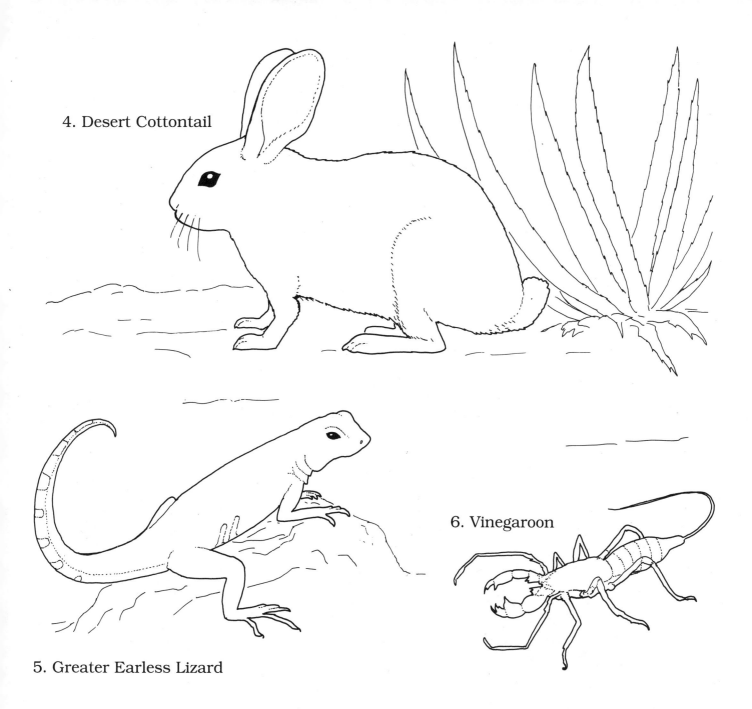

4. Desert Cottontail

5. Greater Earless Lizard

6. Vinegaroon

will even tackle a rattlesnake, thrashing the reptile against a rock until it is dead.

Pioneers from the eastern United States must have thought that the **Desert Cottontail (4),** with its puffy white tail and long ears, looked like rabbits they had seen before. But they probably were not used to seeing so many reptiles.

One of the many lizards found here is the **Greater Earless Lizard (5)**. It likes open areas with room to run. As it dashes from shrub to shrub, it curls its tail up and forward, revealing black and white markings on the underside.

The **Vinegaroon (6)** is another creature that would have amazed early travelers in the

desert. Because of its resemblance to a scorpion, it is sometimes called the whipscorpion. Unlike true scorpions, however, the Vinegaroon cannot sting. It does use the long "whip" on its abdomen to defend itself, however. If threatened, the Vinegaroon aims its whip at a predator and sprays a sour-smelling liquid. Mostly active at night, it spends the day under rocks.

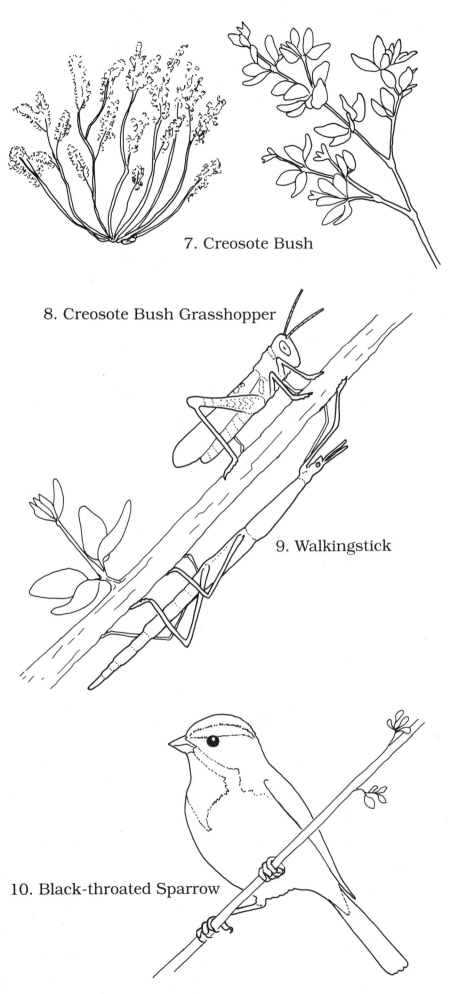

7. Creosote Bush

8. Creosote Bush Grasshopper

9. Walkingstick

10. Black-throated Sparrow

Creosote Bush (7) is a very common desert shrub. In fact, it is found in three of the four North American deserts. Its small green leaves have a waxy coating that helps the plant retain moisture. After a good rain, the leaves have a distinctive odor that many people call the "smell of the desert." Native Americans realized that a plant with such a strong smell must have some medicinal qualities. They used the leaves and branches to treat a variety of ills from stomachaches to snakebites. Creosote Bush is important for wildlife too. Insects feed on it, attracting birds and lizards, which then attract snakes. Many burrowing animals make their dens at the base of the Creosote Bush.

True to its name, the **Creosote Bush Grasshopper (8)** may spend its whole life on the leaves of this bush. Most kinds of grasshoppers will eat many different types of leaves, so this species is unusual in having just one food plant. Since its green color matches the color of these leaves, it is well camouflaged.

Another insect often found on the Creosote Bush is the **Walkingstick (9).** These grayish brown, wingless insects look like twigs, and they are difficult to spot in the branches of the shrubs. The Walkingstick even wavers back and forth when it climbs, looking like a twig blowing in the breeze.

Attracted by the insects, the **Black-throated Sparrow (10)** may be seen perched on top of a Creosote Bush. This handsome bird has a black throat and white stripes on its face. It feeds chiefly on seeds, insects, and some green plants. The Black-throated Sparrow can go a long time without drinking water because it gets enough moisture from the insects and vegetation it eats.

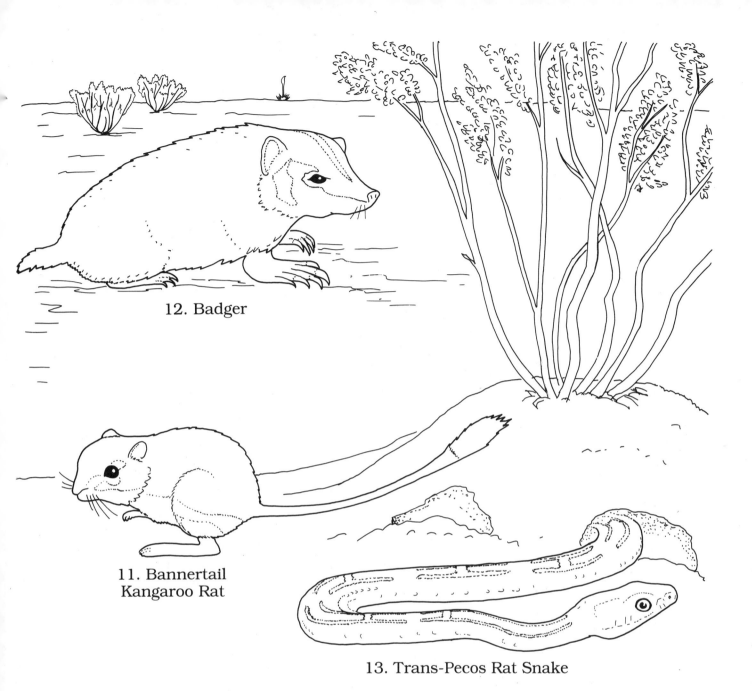

12. Badger

11. Bannertail
Kangaroo Rat

13. Trans-Pecos Rat Snake

The remarkable **Bannertail Kangaroo Rat (11)** does not need to drink water at all. It is able to make its own water from the dry foods, such as seeds, that it eats. Mainly brown in color, the Bannertail Kangaroo Rat has a long tail with white stripes and a distinctive white tip. The tail helps it balance as it hops along like a tiny kangaroo on its big hind feet. The kangaroo rat often nests in a burrow that it digs at the base of a Creosote Bush.

Famous for its digging ability, the **Badger (12)** would like nothing better than to claw its way into the kangaroo rat's burrow. Small rodents are its chief food. The Badger has very long claws on its front feet that help it dig. This heavy-bodied mammal has white cheeks, a white stripe extending from the nose over the top of the head, and black spots in front of each ear. Its belly and tail are yellowish. It is an adaptable animal that lives in many places besides the desert.

Large eyes and a broad head give the **Trans-Pecos Rat Snake (13)** a "bug-eyed" look. It has dark brown H-shaped markings on a yellowish brown body. This snake can reach up to 5 feet in length. It is not venomous and kills its prey by constriction, squeezing it until it dies from suffocation. The Trans-Pecos Rat Snake eats rodents, lizards, and small birds. Chiefly active at night, it spends the day in abandoned rodent burrows.

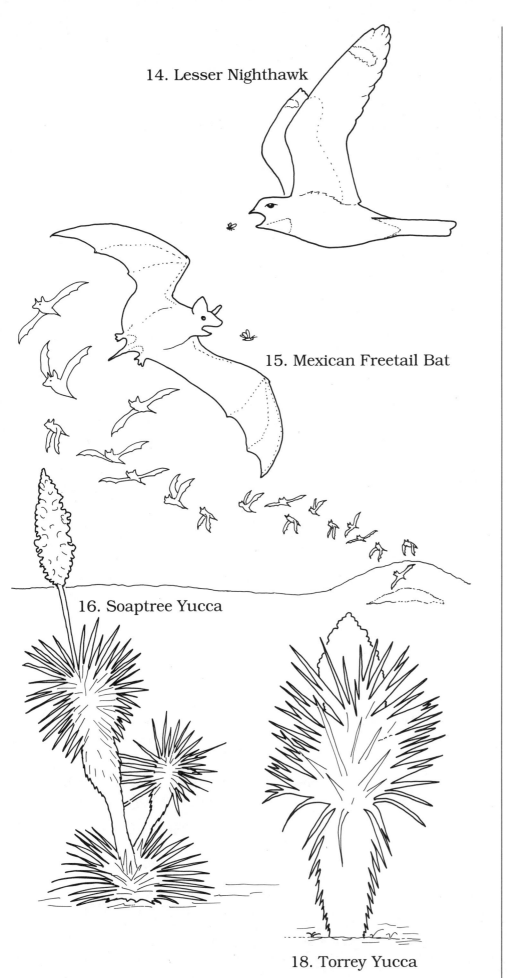

14. Lesser Nighthawk

15. Mexican Freetail Bat

16. Soaptree Yucca

18. Torrey Yucca

With the coming of dusk, the **Lesser Nighthawk (14)** leaves its daytime roosting place and flies in search of moths and other insects. This bird is a graceful flier with narrow, pointed wings. Pale bands across its wingtips may be either white or buffy. During the day it usually sits on the ground where its gray-brown color blends in perfectly with the surroundings.

A spectacular sight is the evening flight of **Mexican Freetail Bats (15).** They live in very large colonies in caves. One cave in Texas has a colony numbering about 20 million bats! At dusk they emerge from their caves in columns that seem to go on forever. Mexican Freetails eat large quantities of insects. The female of this species bears one baby each season. Remarkably, each female can find her own young among all the thousands of baby bats when she returns to the cave.

The **Soaptree Yucca (16)** was an important wild plant for Native American people. Its roots were used to make soap. This distinctive plant has a straight, long flower stalk reaching skyward. The flowers are creamy white in color. They are pollinated by the small white **Pronuba Moth (17)** shown on page 13. This moth flies at dusk when the white flowers of the yucca are easy to see. The female moth flies from yucca flower to yucca flower collecting pollen, which she shapes into a tiny ball. Then she selects a yucca flower in which to lay her eggs. After each egg is laid, the moth deposits some of her collected pollen into the flower. This enables the flower to make seeds, which the moth's offspring eat. This is a good example of how plants and animals depend on one another.

Another yucca of the Chihuahuan Desert is **Torrey Yucca (18).** It has long, sharply pointed, yellow-green leaves and coarse threads along the leaf edges. Its flower stalk is shorter than the Soaptree Yucca. The trunk is often covered by dead brown leaves that help shade the plant from the intense rays of the summer sun. Native Americans made baskets, ropes, and mats from the leaf fibers.

A butterfly that may lay its eggs on almost any kind of yucca is the **Colorado Yucca Borer (19).** The female yucca borer "glues" her eggs to the tips of the leaves. The emerging caterpillars build little silk nests for themselves and eat the yucca leaves. When the caterpillars are older, they will bore tunnels down into the roots of the yucca, living there and eating the roots. The adult butterflies have black uppersides with creamy white spots on the forewings.

The flower stalk of the yucca makes a fine perch for the tiny **Black-chinned Hummingbird (20),** a bird only about 3½ inches long. The male has a black throat or chin. Beneath the black there is a band of purple. In just the right light, these purple feathers are iridescent. Otherwise, this band will just appear dark. The color on the male's throat is a feature for attracting a mate. The male also performs a courtship display, buzzing back and forth in the air in front of the female. The female Black-chinned Hummingbird lays two eggs in a tiny, cuplike nest. Each egg is about the size of a lima bean.

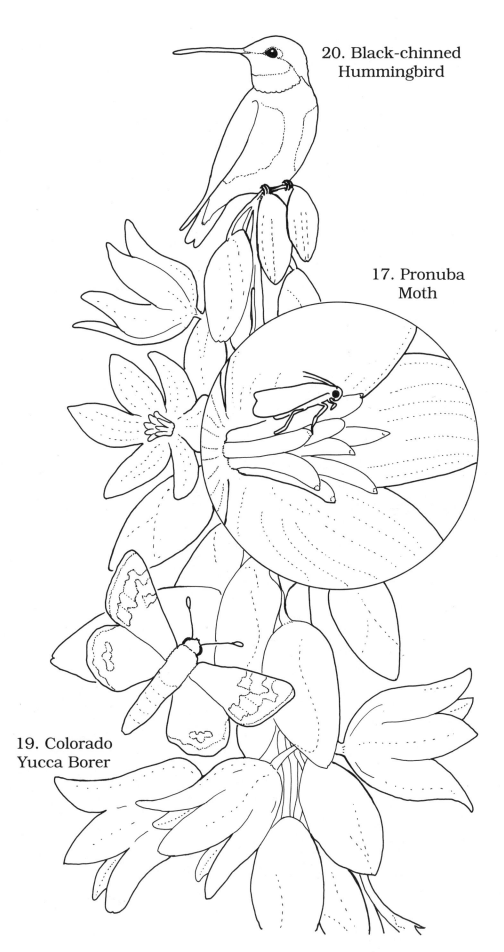

20. Black-chinned Hummingbird

17. Pronuba Moth

19. Colorado Yucca Borer

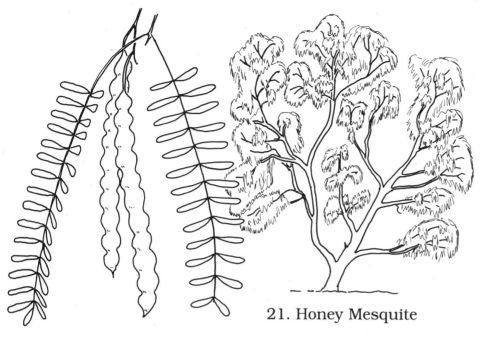

21. Honey Mesquite

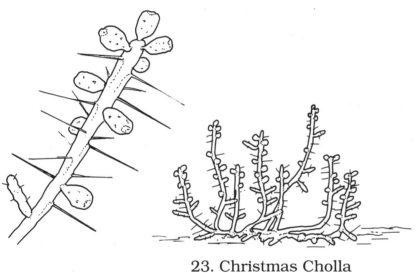

23. Christmas Cholla

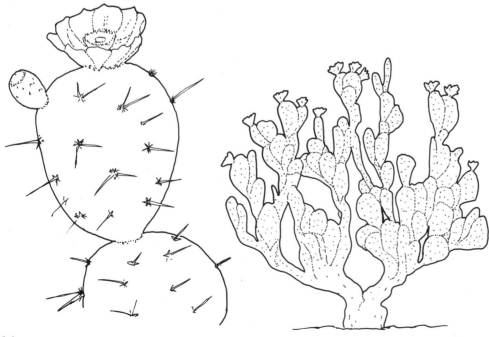

22. Texas Prickly Pear

In a land of few trees, the shade offered by the **Honey Mesquite (21)** is welcome. This tree ranges from 10 to 30 feet high. Mesquites have several strategies for dealing with water shortages. They have long tap roots that can go down 60 feet or more to reach ground water. This gives them a steady supply of moisture even when rainfall is scarce. Also, because their gray-green leaflets are so small, less moisture is lost to evaporation. In the spring, the Honey Mesquite has creamy yellow flower spikes that attract bees. Then come light brown seed pods, which many desert animals eat. The Honey Mesquite is also important because it provides nesting sites for birds.

The **Texas Prickly Pear (22)** has a different strategy for surviving without a constant supply of water. Like other kinds of cactus, this plant is a succulent, meaning it can store water in its large, blue-green pads. Many animals get moisture by eating the pads. Its purple seedy fruit is also popular with birds and animals.

Another type of cactus with the capacity to store water is the **Christmas Cholla (23)** (CHOY-yah). It is so named because it is "decorated" with red fruits that stay on the plant through the winter months. It is bushy and only about 1 or 2 feet tall. Two-inch-long spines jut out from its slender branches.

Almost uniformly brown, the **Crissal Thrasher (24)** has a long curved bill. A closer look reveals a dark reddish brown patch under its tail. This bird forages for food by digging with its heavy bill. For its nest, it makes a cup of thorny twigs,

14

often in a mesquite tree. Its eggs are pale blue-green and unmarked. It has a long start-and-stop song with lots of changes, as if the bird can't decide what to sing.

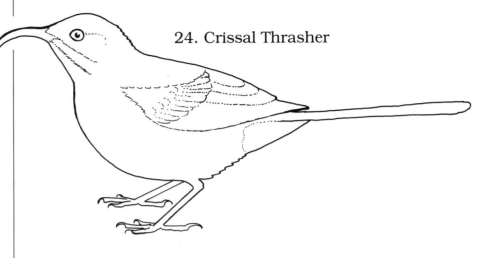

24. Crissal Thrasher

Well camouflaged against a background of desert soil and rocks, the **Texas Horned Lizard (25)** may be hard to spot. Its coloration varies with soil color. Horned lizards are often called "horny toads" because they have broad, toad-shaped bodies, but they are true lizards. The Texas Horned Lizard has a spiny back and two enlarged horns at the back of its head. It preys on harvester ants and may eat as many as 100 ants in a day.

25. Texas Horned Lizard

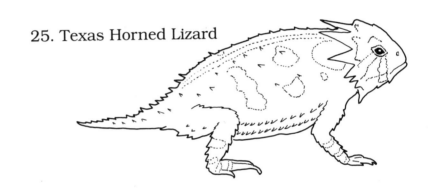

A small relative of the kangaroo rat, the **Desert Pocket Mouse (26)** has coarse, yellowish brown hair and a tail that is longer than its head and body. It prefers open desert with lots of space among the plants. It eats seeds and insects. As it forages, it stuffs the seeds of mesquites and other plants into its cheek pouches to carry them back to its den.

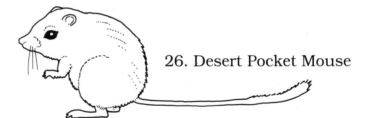

26. Desert Pocket Mouse

The Desert Pocket Mouse must be wary of the secretive **Mexican Kingsnake (27).** This reptile becomes active at night and likes to eat rodents, lizards, frogs, and smaller snakes. It usually has a pattern of gray and red-orange bands.

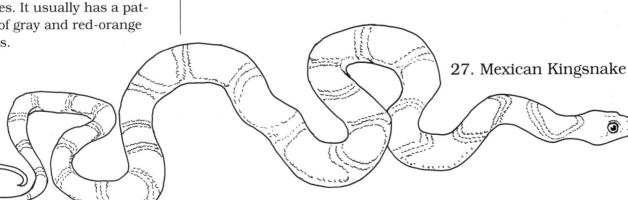

27. Mexican Kingsnake

29. Hognose Skunk

30. Cave Myotis

28. Crevice
Spiny Lizard

31. Texas Lyre Snake

Rocky Places in the Chihuahuan Desert

Many animals prefer rocky areas because the stones provide shade and hiding places. If you visit a rocky hillside in the Chihuahuan Desert, you may see a **Crevice Spiny Lizard (28)** basking on a boulder in the sun. This is a large, flat-bodied lizard with a bold black collar. Sharp-eyed and wary, the Crevice Spiny Lizard may retreat into a crack in the rocks if approached too closely. Its diet consists of insects and some plant buds and leaves.

Though it is most active at night, the **Hognose Skunk (29)** is sometimes seen during the day. It gets its name from its long, piglike snout. The lower sides and belly of this skunk are black, but its entire back and tail are white. The Hognose Skunk is a solitary animal; you usually don't see more than one at a time. For its den, it chooses a safe place among the rocks. It usually produces 2 to 4 young per season. It has long claws for digging, and it uses its naked snout to root for food. It eats insects, small mammals, reptiles, and plants.

Common in southwestern caves, the **Cave Myotis (30)** is a little bat about 4 inches long. It roosts in large colonies, often on vertical rock walls. Sometimes, however, you can find one by itself. In the evening, the bats emerge from their daytime roosts in search of insects, which they catch in midair. The Cave Myotis is drab brown in color.

The **Texas Lyre Snake (31)** gets its name from a faint marking on its head that is the shape of a lyre, a musical instrument like a harp. Its body is gray with blotches of brown. A creature of the night, it eats lizards and small mammals, including bats. During the day it hides in rocky crevices.

Actually a wasp without wings, the female **Velvet Ant (32)** can inflict a painful sting. These insects are usually black with red or orange. Their bright colors may serve to warn predators away. Velvet Ants lay their eggs in the nests of other insects. When the female is ready to lay her eggs, she looks for the nest of a burrowing bee or wasp. She enters the nest, eats some of the pollen and nectar that the host has gathered, lays an egg, and then leaves. When the egg hatches, the Velvet Ant larva eats not only the food stored in the nest but also the larvae of the host insect.

If you turn over a rock or piece of wood, you may find a black or brown wormlike creature called a **millipede (33).** Its body has many segments, with two pairs of tiny legs attached to each segment (its name means "a thousand feet"). In the desert, millipedes are usually seen after a rain, so people sometimes call them "rainworms." They have chewing mouthparts and eat live and dead plants.

Another rock dweller is the **Texas Banded Gecko (34).** Active only at night, it emerges from its rocky hiding place to hunt insects and small spiders, twitching its tail like a cat as it stalks its prey. Its white-rimmed eyelids give it a sleepy expression. It is yellow or pink in color with dark brown spots or bands. This gecko squeaks when it is alarmed.

32. Velvet Ant

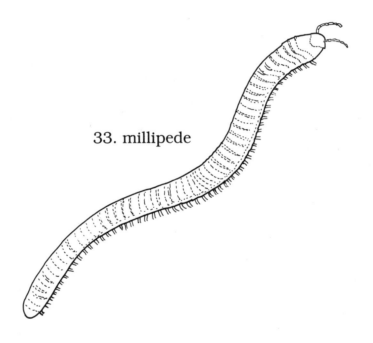

33. millipede

34. Texas Banded Gecko

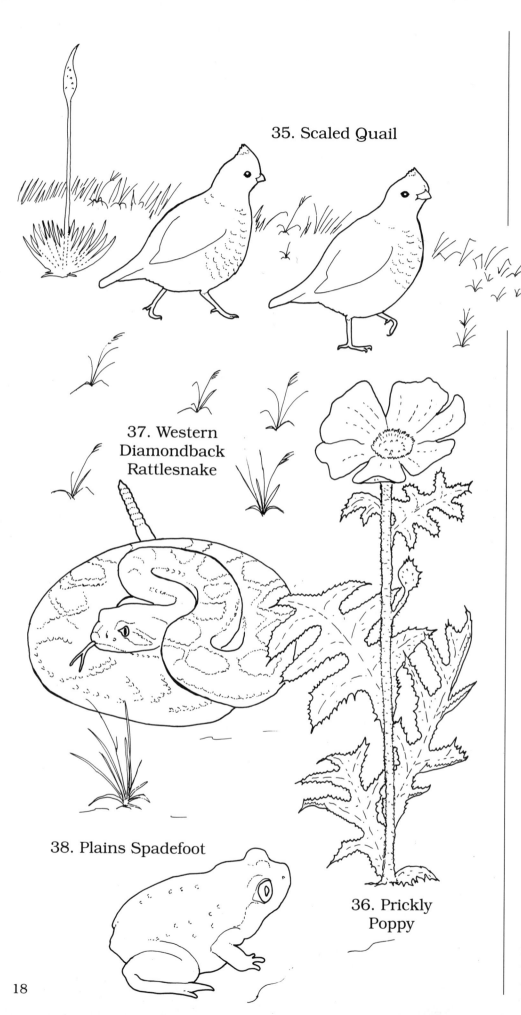

35. Scaled Quail

37. Western
Diamondback
Rattlesnake

38. Plains Spadefoot

36. Prickly
Poppy

In Texas and New Mexico the Great Plains merge into the dry desert grassland areas of the Chihuahuan Desert. A bird that is widespread here is the **Scaled Quail (35).** Pale gray with scaly markings on its breast and back, it has a bushy white crest. This is why it is often called "cotton top." Like the Roadrunner, this bird prefers to run rather than fly. For its nest it makes a hollow depression under a bush and lines it with dry grass.

The **Prickly Poppy (36)** is named for its prickly stems and leaves. Some people also call it "cowboy's fried egg" because it has large white flowers with yellow centers.

Largest of the western rattlers, the **Western Diamondback Rattlesnake (37)** is a wary, defensive reptile. It may be the most dangerous North American snake because it often would rather fight than flee, and its bite can be fatal. It can grow to be 4 to 7 feet long. It is named for the brown diamond-shaped patches along its back. When threatened, it vibrates the rattle at the end of its tail, making a loud buzzing sound.

A toad that likes the desert grasslands is the **Plains Spadefoot (38).** Only a couple of inches long, this species has a prominent bony hump between its eyes. Toads need water to breed in, so in the Chihuahuan Desert, breeding takes place in the short rainy season in July. When the rains come and shallow ponds begin to fill, male spadefoots gather at night near the water and call to attract females, singing a chorus of short quacks. The females lay as many as 200 eggs each in shallow ponds, and the eggs hatch within 48 hours. The Plains Spadefoot prefers loose, sandy or gravelly soil for burrowing underground.

Another bird found in open grasslands is the **Swainson's Hawk (39).** It may soar high overhead as it searches for food, such as small mammals, snakes, lizards, large insects, and young birds. Like some other hawks, it may be any of several different colorations. Swainson's Hawk spends the winter in southern South America but returns to North America in the spring, often migrating in large flocks.

If you hear a snapping sound in the grasslands, it may be the **Horse Lubber Grasshopper (40).** The males of this species make a loud noise by snapping their forewings together. The Horse Lubber is shiny black with contrasting orange or yellow markings. When disturbed, it may flit from bush to bush.

A trailing vine with very long stems, the **Buffalo Gourd (41)** has yellow, trumpet-shaped blossoms. The flowers are replaced by striped green fruits about the size of a tennis ball. Native Americans sometimes cooked the seeds of the Buffalo Gourd into a mush.

The **Texas Blind Snake (42)** is an odd reptile that looks more like a large earthworm. It prefers loose, damp soil where it can burrow below the surface out of the sun. At night it comes out to search for food — primarily ants and termites. Its tough, hard scales protect it from ant bites when it crawls into ant nests.

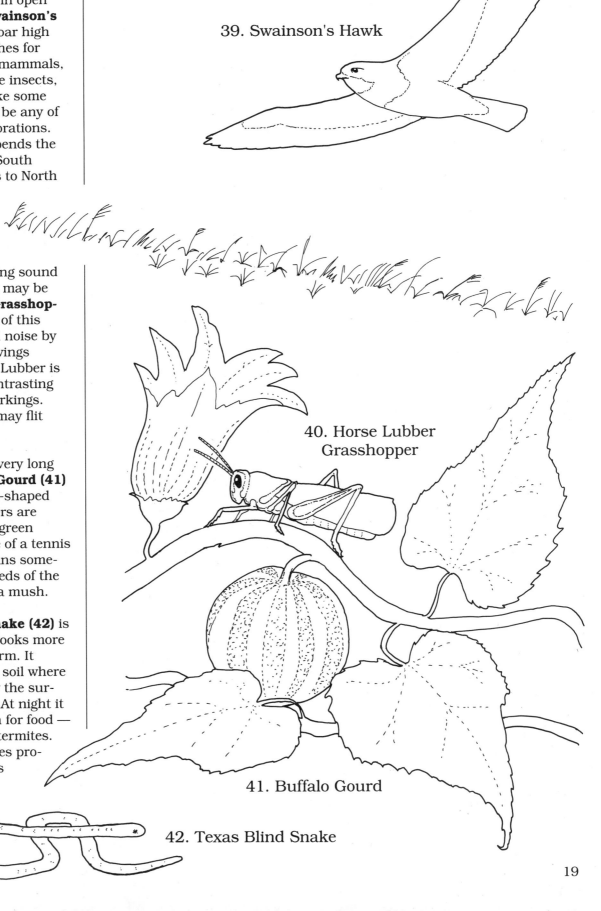

39. Swainson's Hawk

40. Horse Lubber Grasshopper

41. Buffalo Gourd

42. Texas Blind Snake

Desert Canyons

Over time, the action of wind, rain, sand, and running water has carved canyons in some places in our deserts. Streams may run here for a short time after occasional heavy rains. The water usually disappears in a few days, perhaps leaving behind a pool or two.

A tree that often grows in desert canyons, mainly in the Sonoran Desert, is the **Arizona Sycamore (43).** Its green leaves are large and shaped like the leaves on a maple tree, and its smooth bark is whitish with pale brown patches. Another way to recognize this plant is by the brown "buttonball" fruits, which stay on the tree even after it has dropped all of its leaves. Arizona Sycamores can grow to 80 feet tall, and their trunks can be 2 to 5 feet in diameter. The roots often wrap around streambed boulders.

The black and lemon yellow **Scott's Oriole (44)** is often seen in the sycamores and other trees in the canyons. The nest of this bird is a grassy pouch usually built in a yucca or small tree. This oriole will sip nectar from flowers such as those of the agave shown on page 21. It also feeds on insects and fruit.

A large mammal with a long tail climbing a tree is likely to be the **Coatimundi (45)** (coh-AH-tee-MOON-dee), or Coati. It has a long whitish nose and white spots above and below each eye. This tropical animal enters the United States only in canyon country near the Mexican border. Several Coatis may prowl the canyon in an active troop, especially at night. They use their long snouts to root for grubs and roots, and they also like to eat fruit, nuts, lizards, and scorpions.

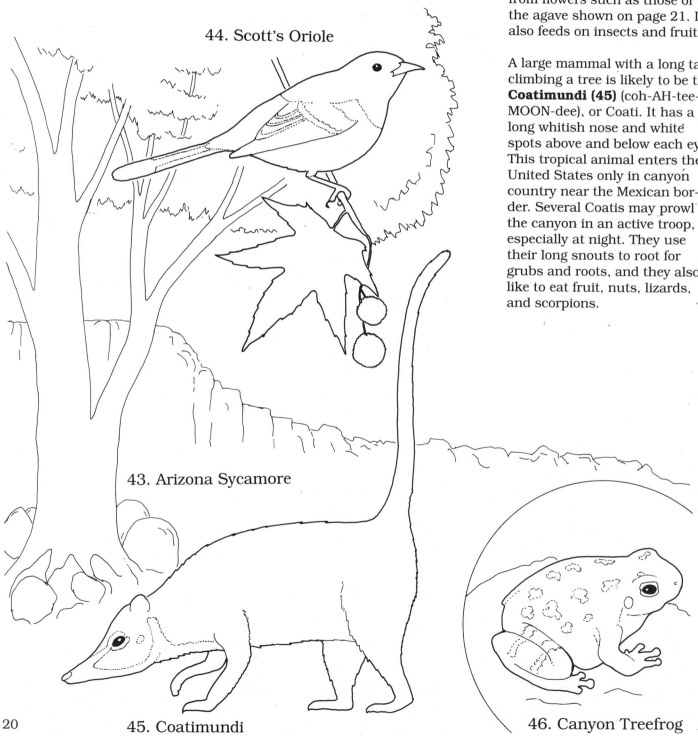

44. Scott's Oriole

43. Arizona Sycamore

45. Coatimundi

46. Canyon Treefrog

The **Canyon Treefrog (46)** lives in rocky ravines. It usually stays on the ground but sometimes climbs trees. It is a blotchy gray-brown or olive, good camouflage among the rocks and boulders. The Canyon Treefrog is only 2 inches long, but it is loud for its size. Listen for its hoarse, trilling call.

The **Ringtail (47)** gets its name from the black and white rings on its bushy tail. Its body is yellowish gray, and it has big eyes, big ears, and a pointed nose. This is a shy, nocturnal animal that comes out at night in search of mice, woodrats, grasshoppers, and berries. It makes its den among large boulders near the canyon floor.

Palmer's Agave (48) often grows on the rocky slopes of desert canyons. The long flower stalk of this plant rises from a clump of succulent green leaves. The stalks grow very quickly and produce many flowers and seeds. The showy displays of yellow flowers attract insects, hummingbirds, and nectar-feeding bats.

If you are very lucky, you may see a male **Lucifer Hummingbird (49)** hovering at the blossoms of the agave. This uncommon hummingbird has a purple throat, green crown and back, and curved bill. It feeds on insects as well as nectar.

Higher up in the canyon, the sure-footed **Desert Bighorn (50)** makes its way over the rocks and boulders. These magnificent creatures have massive coiled horns. Their bodies are mostly grayish brown. Bighorns are wary and have a keen sense of sight for detecting danger. They are well adapted to rocky ranges, for they are able to leap and climb up and down steep cliffs and can go a long time without water.

50. Desert Bighorn

49. Lucifer Hummingbird

47. Ringtail

48. Palmer's Agave

52. Sagebrush Checkerspot

The Great Basin

Zane Grey, the western novelist, described the cowboys in his stories riding out of town onto the sagebrush plains. He was writing about the Great Basin Desert, and his description of this more northerly desert was a good one. There are few trees or succulents here; instead, the landscape is dotted with low-growing shrubs. Sagebrush is by far the most important of these shrubs. Because it is so abundant, the open country in this region is often called "sageland" or sagebrush country. Many of the common plants and animals that live here have sage or sagebrush as part of their names.

Big Sagebrush (51) is the popular symbol of the Great Basin Desert. It has grayish green, three-lobed leaves that are very fragrant. One reason Big Sagebrush is such a successful plant is that it has a double root system, just like the Creosote Bush, which is so common in the other three deserts. It has shallow roots close to the surface of the ground in order to readily collect rainwater. In addition, it has deep, penetrating roots that seek out moisture from farther underground.

Patterned with orange, black, and white lines, the **Sagebrush Checkerspot (52)** is a butterfly found all over the Great Basin Desert and up into the surrounding mountains. Its caterpillars feed on a shrub called rabbitbrush. Adult Checkerspots visit flowers and also are attracted to the muddy edges of puddles.

51. Big Sagebrush

Although Big Sagebrush is usually the most common type, several other kinds of sagebrush are found in the Great Basin. So named because it prefers sandy soil, **Sand Sagebrush (53)** looks like Big Sagebrush but is smaller and has thinner leaves. Sagebrush leaves, stems, and buds are eaten by antelope, deer, and birds. These shrubs also provide places to nest and hide for a variety of animals.

The **Sagebrush Lizard (54)** lives mostly on the ground but may climb up into bushes when it is frightened. It may be seen during the day when it is out searching for insects and spiders to eat. Although its back is not very colorful, the Sagebrush Lizard has a rust-colored spot just behind the front legs. The male usually has blue patches on his throat and belly.

The **Sage Grouse (55)** is thoroughly at home in this habitat. It builds its nest under sagebrush shrubs and feeds on sage buds and leaves. The male is unmistakable, with his black belly patch, black throat, spiky tail feathers, and large size (he is more than 2 feet long). His courtship display is a spectacular sight in the spring. He puffs out his chest, raises and spreads his tail, and makes a loud popping sound during this ritual.

53. Sand Sagebrush

54. Sagebrush Lizard

55. Sage Grouse

23

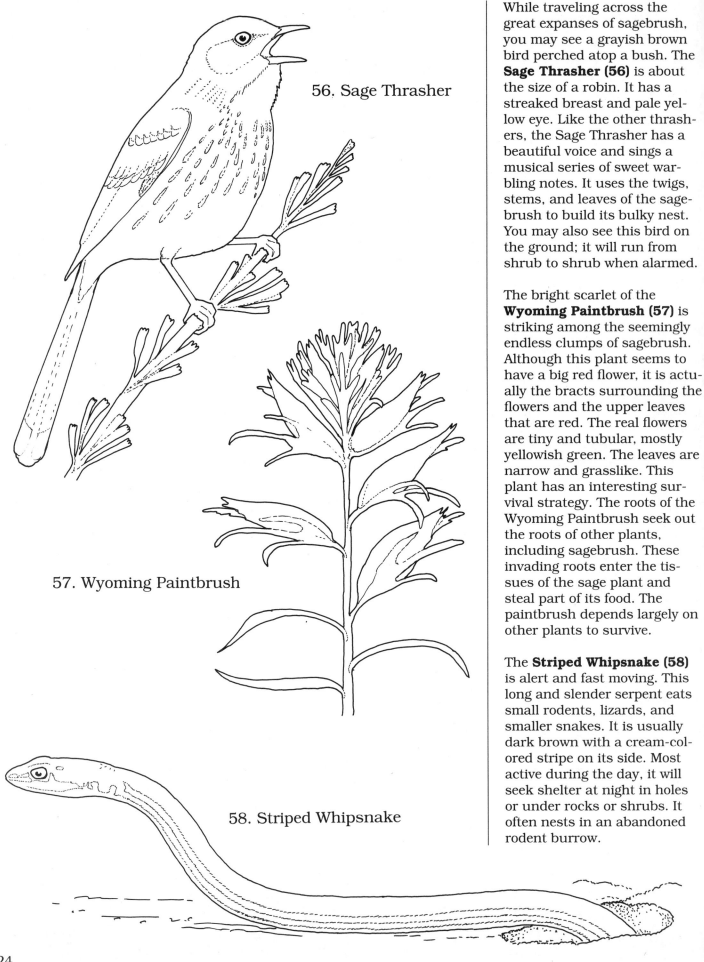

56. Sage Thrasher

57. Wyoming Paintbrush

58. Striped Whipsnake

While traveling across the great expanses of sagebrush, you may see a grayish brown bird perched atop a bush. The **Sage Thrasher (56)** is about the size of a robin. It has a streaked breast and pale yellow eye. Like the other thrashers, the Sage Thrasher has a beautiful voice and sings a musical series of sweet warbling notes. It uses the twigs, stems, and leaves of the sagebrush to build its bulky nest. You may also see this bird on the ground; it will run from shrub to shrub when alarmed.

The bright scarlet of the **Wyoming Paintbrush (57)** is striking among the seemingly endless clumps of sagebrush. Although this plant seems to have a big red flower, it is actually the bracts surrounding the flowers and the upper leaves that are red. The real flowers are tiny and tubular, mostly yellowish green. The leaves are narrow and grasslike. This plant has an interesting survival strategy. The roots of the Wyoming Paintbrush seek out the roots of other plants, including sagebrush. These invading roots enter the tissues of the sage plant and steal part of its food. The paintbrush depends largely on other plants to survive.

The **Striped Whipsnake (58)** is alert and fast moving. This long and slender serpent eats small rodents, lizards, and smaller snakes. It is usually dark brown with a cream-colored stripe on its side. Most active during the day, it will seek shelter at night in holes or under rocks or shrubs. It often nests in an abandoned rodent burrow.

A widespread insect that is at home in the desert is the **Mormon Cricket (59).** It was named after thousands of these crickets attacked the first crops of the Mormon pioneers in 1848. It feeds primarily on sagebrush and grains. Dark brown in color, the Mormon Cricket's antennae are as long as its body. It makes a rapid trilling or hoarse chirping sound. Adult females deposit eggs below the surface of the soil in midsummer, and the eggs hatch the following spring.

With its stiff, upright, blue-green stems, **Mormon Tea (60)** is a distinctive looking plant. It may be 2 to 5 feet tall. Native Americans, Spanish explorers, and early settlers used the dried stems of this plant to make a tea. The tea was thought to have medicinal properties.

Carefully hidden within a sage plant, the nest of the **Sage Sparrow (61)** is difficult to spot. Gray with a single dark blotch on its breast, this sparrow has dark "whiskers" on the sides of its throat. Its nest is built of shreds of sage bark and twigs and then lined with soft, dry grass. The female lays 3 or 4 pale blue, speckled eggs. Although some sparrows hop, the Sage Sparrow runs on the ground with its tail held up in the air. It has a tinkling, musical song.

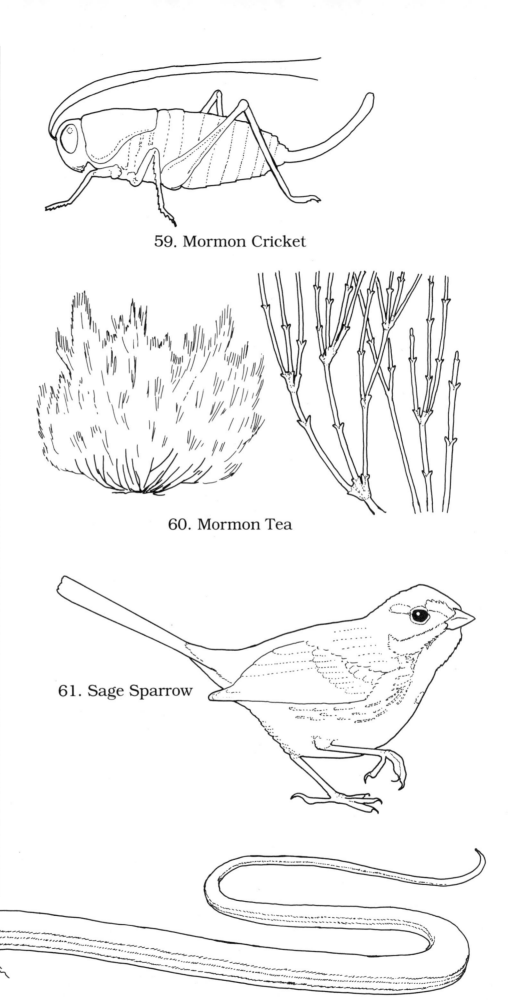

59. Mormon Cricket

60. Mormon Tea

61. Sage Sparrow

25

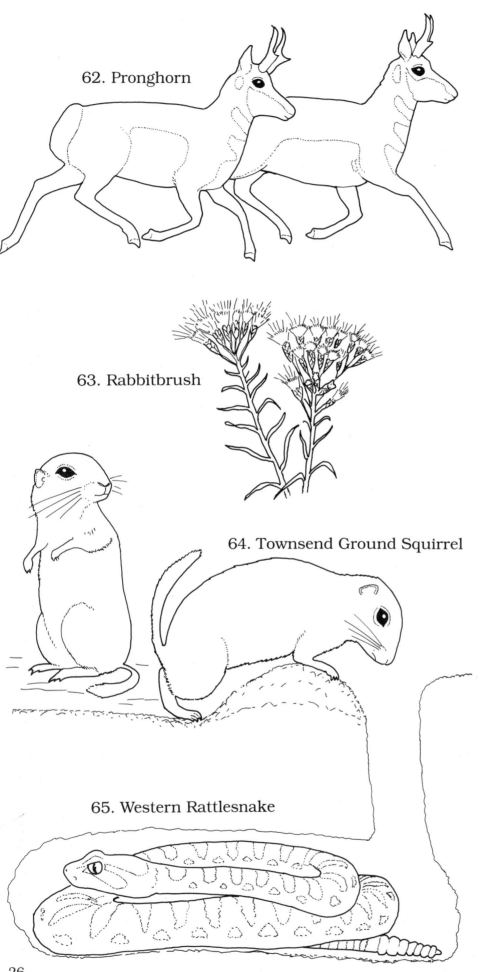

62. Pronghorn

63. Rabbitbrush

64. Townsend Ground Squirrel

65. Western Rattlesnake

Small bands of **Pronghorn (62)** roam the sagebrush plains of the Great Basin. These animals are sometimes called "pronghorn antelope," but they are not really antelope at all. They are easily recognized by the large white rump patch, white lower sides, and two broad white bands across the neck. These sleek animals can run for exceptionally long distances; they can keep going at about 40 miles per hour for up to 15 minutes. At one time, they may have needed this speed and endurance to escape from packs of wolves that roamed the West. Pronghorns are most active in the morning and evening. They feed on sagebrush and many different kinds of weeds and some grasses.

One food plant of the Pronghorn is a yellow-flowered shrub called **Rabbitbrush (63).** Like all other plants and animals, Rabbitbrush also has a scientific name: *Chrysothamnus nauseosus*. Originally taken from the Greek language, *Chrysothamnus* means "golden shrub" and *nauseosus* means "heavy-scented."

Townsend Ground Squirrels (64) dig burrows in the ground and spend lots of time scurrying in and out of them. Their underground tunnels provide protection from predators and from unfavorable weather conditions. These short-tailed, smoky gray rodents feed on green plants and seeds.

A snake that may be found in the Great Basin brushland is the venomous **Western Rattlesnake (65).** It is a blotchy brown color and has subtle dark and light rings on its tail. Like other rattlesnakes, it has a series of rattles at the end of its tail. These are loosely connected segments made of a stiff, hornlike material. When the snake is alarmed, it shakes its tail, and the segments rattle against each other. Western Rattlesnakes often seek shelter in mammal burrows.

Red-tailed Hawks (66) are found all over North America, but they are abundant in open areas of the West, including the Great Basin. They soar in the sky as they search for prey, especially rodents, which are their main source of food. Adult Red-tails often have reddish upper tails and dark belly bands, but there are many variations in color. The male and female birds work together to make a nest of sticks and twigs. They usually raise two or three young hawks each summer.

The **Mormon Metalmark (67)** is a butterfly that feeds on nectar, especially at the flowers of various kinds of buckwheat. The upper sides of the wings are orange-brown with white and black spots. The female lays clusters of pale pink eggs on the dry, lower leaves of the Sulphur Flower or another kind of buckwheat, and the eggs hatch out into tiny caterpillars. In the picture here, two little purple Metalmark caterpillars are resting on the stems of the Sulphur Flower. But in real life, these caterpillars usually hide by day and feed at night.

The seeds of the **Sulphur Flower (68)** are a major food source for the ground squirrels and for seed-eating birds. This plant is a member of the buckwheat family. It has leafless flower stalks that rise out of a cluster of leaves and branches. The flowers are yellow or cream-colored.

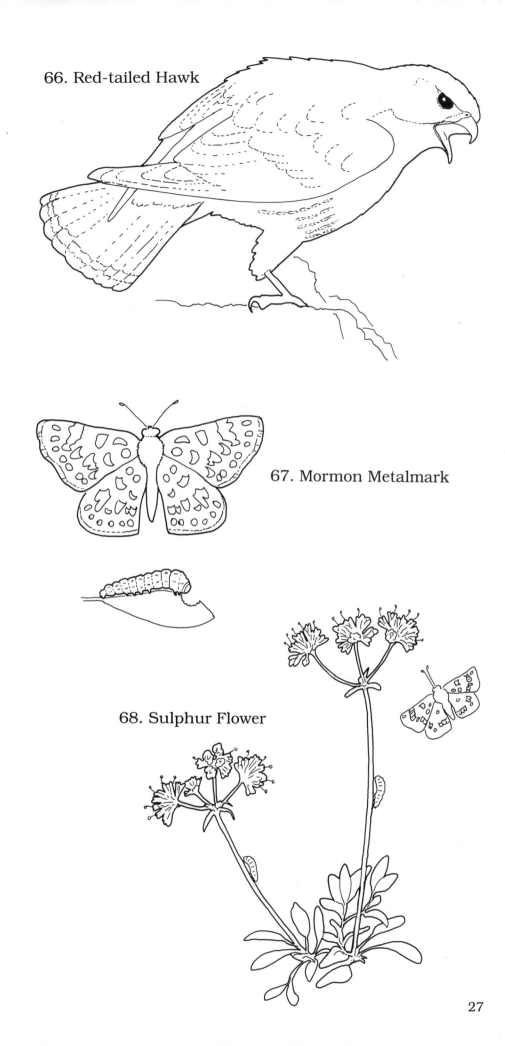

66. Red-tailed Hawk

67. Mormon Metalmark

68. Sulphur Flower

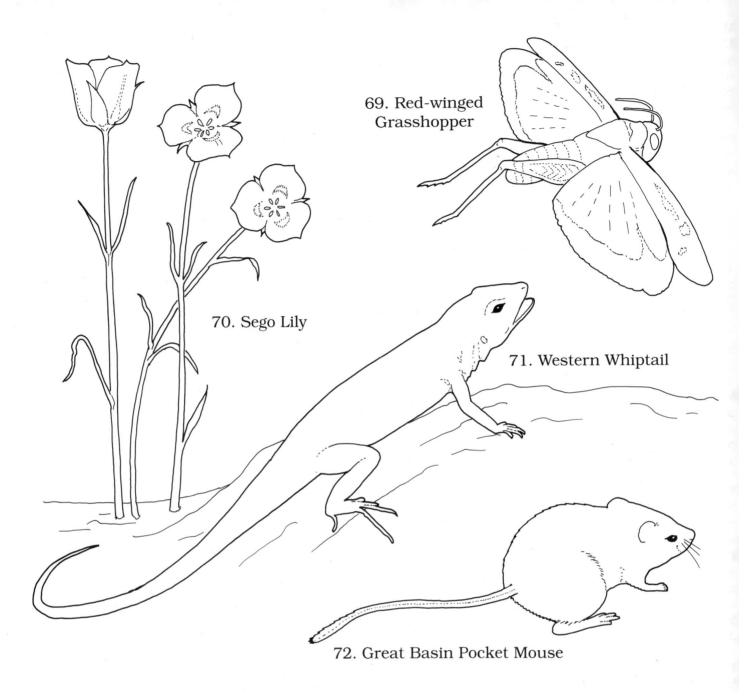

69. Red-winged Grasshopper

70. Sego Lily

71. Western Whiptail

72. Great Basin Pocket Mouse

True to its name, the **Red-winged Grasshopper (69)** has bright red hind wings with black edges. This insect makes short flights a few feet above the ground. As it flies, it makes a loud crackling noise. This rattling crackle, along with the brightly colored wings, make it very noticeable. These grasshoppers are widespread and can be found in other places besides the desert.

A plant to look for among the sagebrush is the **Sego Lily (70),** the state flower of Utah. It has white, cup-shaped flowers. The bases of the flower petals are yellow with purple spots. The slender stem has a few grasslike leaves. This plant has a large, fat root, tasting much like a potato, that Native Americans used to eat.

Preferring open areas where there is lots of room to run, the **Western Whiptail (71)** is an active, speedy lizard. In fact, speed is probably its most valuable asset for escaping predators. This lizard is found in many parts of the West, and its markings vary from place to place. In the Great Basin, it has four light stripes on its back. It moves with jerky steps as it searches for insects to eat.

Common in sagebrush country, the **Great Basin Pocket Mouse (72)** feeds mainly on seeds, which it stores in its den. It may also eat caterpillars. Like many other desert animals, this pocket mouse rarely drinks but gets most of its water from the food it eats. The Great Basin Pocket Mouse is buffy colored with a long tail. It makes burrows underneath shrubs.

Winter in the Great Basin Desert can be cold and even snowy. Some animals hibernate through the cold months, others remain active; still others migrate to warmer climates.

Often heard before it is seen, the **Common Raven (73)** has a harsh, croaking call. This large, all-black bird does not migrate but stays in the Great Basin in winter. It survives because of its adaptable diet: it eats almost anything. Ravens are skilled flyers and seem playful at times as they swoop through the air.

If you see a short-tailed gray mouse running on the ground in sagebrush country, it is likely to be the **Sagebrush Vole (74).** Because of the year-round availability of sage, its main source of food, the Sagebrush Vole is able to remain active even through the winter.

A good plant food for pronghorn and other browsing animals is a small, grayish white shrub called **Winter Fat (75).** The name comes from its importance as a winter grazing plant when other food is scarce. Although its leaves dry out in fall, they remain on the plant for much of the winter.

The **Short-horned Lizard (76)** has short horns separated by a wide notch. It can stand colder weather than other horned lizards. Other kinds of horned lizards lay eggs and bury them in the ground, and sunlight warming the soil helps the eggs to hatch. But the Short-horned Lizard lives in places where the soil may not be dependably warm in summer; so instead of laying eggs, it bears live young. It may produce as many as 20 offspring. Remarkably, the tiny newborns become fully active within about 30 minutes of birth. From that time on, they are on their own.

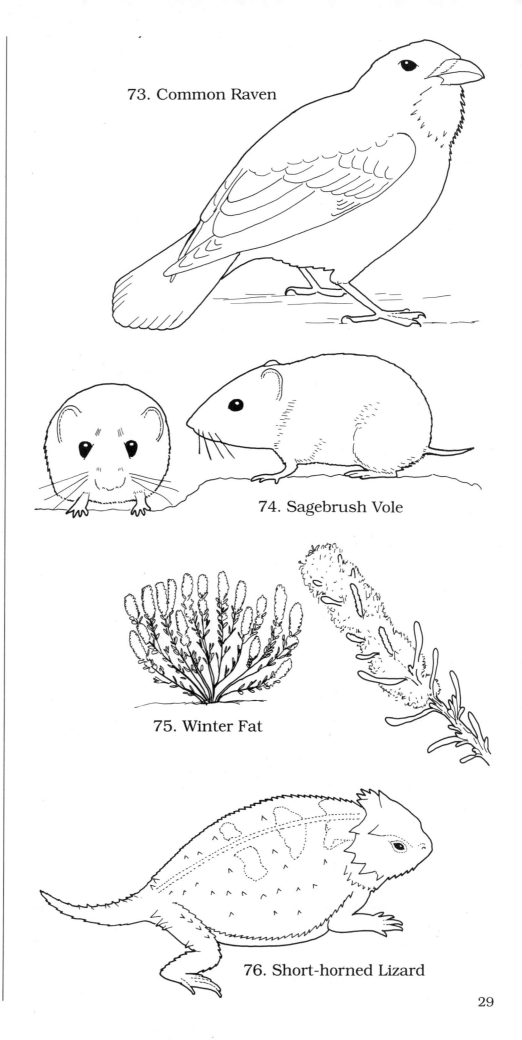

73. Common Raven

74. Sagebrush Vole

75. Winter Fat

76. Short-horned Lizard

29

Night in the Great Basin

As night falls, the animals that were active during the day return to their roosts, but this does not mean that all is still in the Great Basin Desert at night. A whole new cast of characters emerges as darkness descends.

There are many more kinds of moths than butterflies, but we are less likely to notice moths because many of them are small and are active only at night. The **Green Geometer (77)** moth is common over a large part of the West. The adults are pale green with white stripes. The caterpillars of the Green Geometer feed on the flowers and buds of a variety of desert plants.

Prowling through the darkness in search of frogs, toads, and lizards, the **Night Snake (78)** is gray or tan with dark spots. It usually has larger dark blotches on each side of its neck. This slender snake can be anywhere from 12 to 26 inches long. It kills its prey by injecting venom with teeth located at the back of its jaw, but these snakes are not dangerous to people. During the day, you might uncover one under a rock or other hiding place.

The **Great Basin Spadefoot (79)** is a toad that spends most of the time underground. Using the wedge-shaped "spades" on its hind feet, it can dig down beneath the surface of the soil very quickly. During dry weather, it stays underground, emerging to breed after the rains in midsummer. Occasionally it may come out during the day to hunt for insects, but it is mainly a creature of the night. Its call is a hoarse *wa-wa-wa*.

Emerging well after dark, the rare **Spotted Bat (80)** gives a loud, high-pitched call. This bat has huge ears that are aimed forward as it flies. It gets its name from the large white spots on its shoulders and back.

The **Common Poorwill (81)** gives its repeated, whistled cry, *poor will, poor will,* and then begins its nightly search for moths and other insects. This bird sleeps in the daytime, and it may sleep for most of the winter as well, because this is one of the very few birds known to hibernate. The poorwill is mainly mottled gray-brown with a white throat and white corners to its rounded tail.

Another mammal active at night is the **Great Basin Kangaroo Rat (82)**. It is olive-gray and has a large head. It eats many green leaves, including sagebrush. Well suited to dry environments, it does not have to drink water. This solitary animal relies on protective coloration and speed to avoid predators.

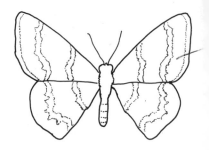

77. Green Geometer

The kangaroo rat is a favorite food of the small and slender **Kit Fox (83)**. With large ears and a black-tipped tail, the Kit Fox is easy to recognize. This mammal has a keen sense of sight, and its big ears are superb for detecting prey in the darkness. In addition to kangaroo rats, it eats other rodents, lizards, insects, and berries. It is unlikely that you will see a Kit Fox during the day, for they spend the daylight hours in their burrows. But if you are riding down a back desert road at night, you may be lucky enough to see the eyeshine of one of these animals, reflecting off the headlights of your car.

79. Great Basin Spadefoot

78. Night Snake

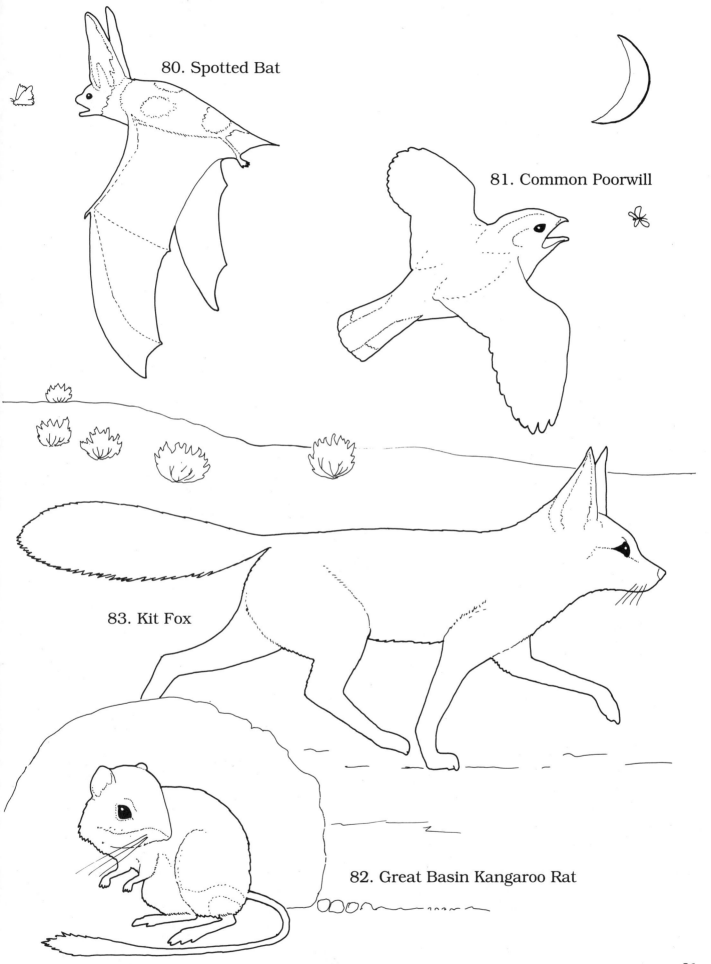

80. Spotted Bat

81. Common Poorwill

83. Kit Fox

82. Great Basin Kangaroo Rat

31

84. Golden Eagle

85. Blacktail Jackrabbit

86. Mule Deer

With a wing span of 7 feet, a large, dark brown bird soars above the desert plains. When it turns just right, you may see a gold sheen on the back of its neck. This is the majestic **Golden Eagle (84).** Suddenly i swoops downward, because it has spotted its favorite prey — a jackrabbit.

The unsuspecting **Blacktail Jackrabbit (85)** has been feeding on a clump of grass. Its long, black-tipped ears continually swivel, listening for sounds of danger. Now the jackrabbit suddenly sits upright and then bounds off to the cover of a sagebrush. Its powerful hind legs let it dash to safety at a speed of up to 35 miles per hour. When the eagle arrives, the only sign of the jackrabbit is its black tail disappearing into the brush.

Another browsing animal of the Great Basin is the **Mule Deer (86).** This is an adaptable mammal that lives in many habitats besides the desert. It is brown with a whitish rump and a black tip to its tail. Mule Deer have large ears, which they seem to move constantly. Adult males of this species can weigh anywhere from 125 to 400 pounds. A remarkable feature of baby Mule Deer is their ability to stand up and walk within a few minutes after they are born.

The Great Basin was not always a desert. Thousands of years ago, much of the land was covered by lakes. After the last Ice Age, the climate became drier, and the lakes began to evaporate. As the waters dried up, the soil became salty. Many plants cannot grow well in salty conditions, but **Greasewood (87)** is one plant that thrives among the salt flats here. It has whitish bark and narrow, bright green leaves. Greasewood provides shelter for many small animals. Its leaves are a source of food for jackrabbits and other creatures.

The **Horned Lark (88),** a bird that lives on open ground, is found in many parts of Europe, Asia, and North America, including the salt flats of the Great Basin. From the back it looks quite dull, but its head pattern is striking. The face and throat are yellow with a black bib below. It also has black whiskers and two black "horns" that are actually feathers sticking up from the sides of its head. These birds are usually found in flocks in winter. If you are in the range of the Horned Lark in the springtime, you may be lucky enough to see the male perform his aerial courtship display. While singing, he will fly very high into the air, circle around, and then dive toward the ground.

Abundant in arid regions of the West, the small brownish **Side-blotched Lizard (89)** spends most of its time on the ground searching for insects, scorpions, spiders, and ticks. It is active mainly during the day. It usually has a dark blotch on its side, but not always. This lizard seeks shelter from predators and from very hot or cold temperatures by going into rodent burrows or under rocks.

The Great Basin has few succulents, but one cactus that grows here is the **Plains Prickly Pear (90).** This low-growing cactus forms clumps only 3 to 6 inches tall. The pads are blue-green in color, with spines 2 to 3 inches long. The spines help protect the plant from hungry animals.

87. Greasewood

88. Horned Lark

89. Side-blotched Lizard

90. Plains Prickly Pear

91. California Washingtonia

Palm Oases

Palm trees may seem out of place in the desert, but they do live in a few canyons in the Mojave and Sonoran Deserts. A palm oasis (plural: oases) may form around a spring or water seep. The water and the shade provided by the trees make the oasis a gathering point for many birds and animals.

The dominant palm tree in a desert oasis is the **California Washingtonia (91),** or fan palm. These trees grow only where water is available at all times of the year. The Washingtonia can be 20 to 75 feet tall and has an unbranched trunk. The green fan-shaped leaves are 5 to 6 feet long. Dead palm fronds usually stay on the tree and form a brown skirt around the trunk. This palm produces black fruits that provide food for a number of species.

The leaves of the palm provide excellent nesting sites for the **Hooded Oriole (92).** The male of this species is bright orange and black, while the female is mostly greenish yellow. The Hooded Oriole builds a pouched nest on the underside of a palm frond. Using palm leaf fibers, it "sews" them together to make the nest secure against even the strongest of winds. The orioles also eat the fruit of the palms.

House Finches (93) are attracted to the seed-filled fruits after they ripen. These birds are streaky brown, and males have red on the breast, rump, forehead, and eyeline. Abundant in desert country, House Finches are social birds and are usually found in small groups.

A large, shiny, dark brown beetle that can be found around the fan palms is the **California Palm Borer (94).** Its young feed on the wood of decaying palms by boring into the wood.

The **Western Yellow Bat (95)** also finds a use for the palm trees. During the day, it sleeps hanging upside down beneath the dead palm fronds. It emerges late in the evening to feed on flying insects. Like many bats, the Western Yellow Bat can find things in the dark by using sonar. It makes high-pitched sounds and listens to the patterns of the echoes. As the name suggests, this bat has yellowish fur.

Fruit knocked off by the House Finches is one source of food for the **Desert Woodrat (96),** which will also eat seeds, berries, and bits of cactus. The woodrat may use dead palm leaves as cover for its nest. Like other "pack-rats," it lives in a large mound of rubbish it builds on the ground.

Listen for the odd quacking sound of the **California Treefrog (97)** in the palm oasis. This is a good location for the treefrog because it likes shady places and quiet pools of permanent water. These frogs are gray with dark blotches. They quickly jump into the water if disturbed but return to shore after the danger has passed.

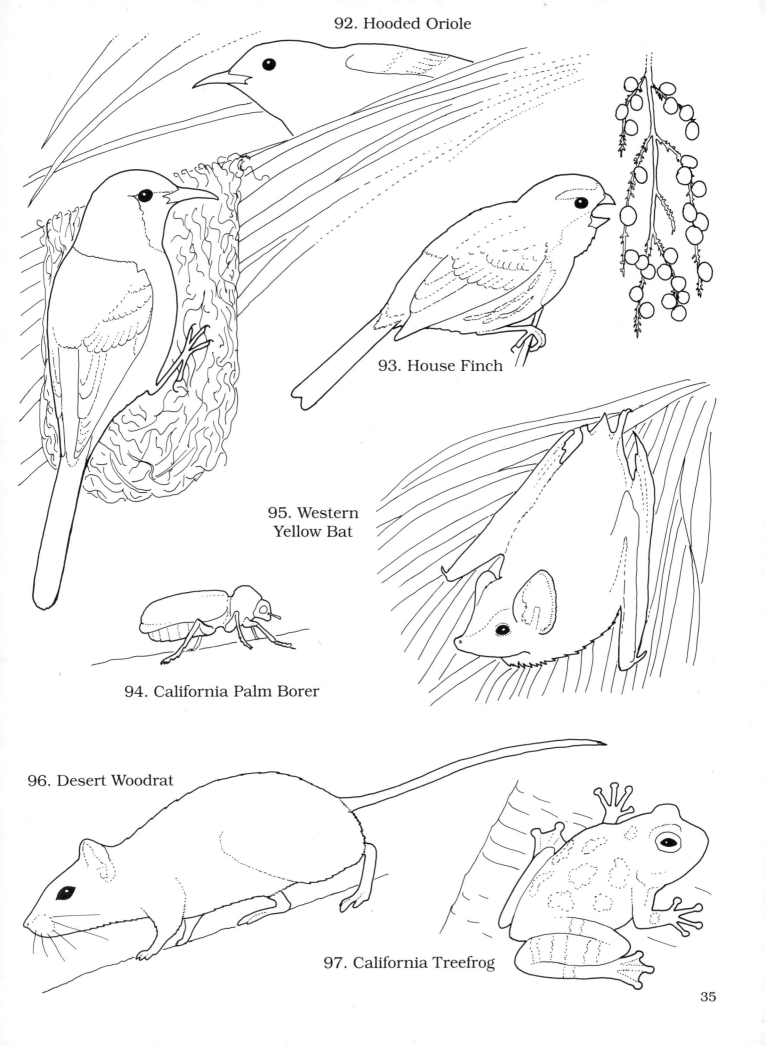

92. Hooded Oriole

93. House Finch

95. Western
Yellow Bat

94. California Palm Borer

96. Desert Woodrat

97. California Treefrog

35

The Mojave Desert

The smallest and driest of the North American deserts is the Mojave. Although the elevation of most of this desert is between 2,000 and 5,000 feet, the Mojave also stakes claim to Death Valley, which is 282 feet below sea level at its lowest point. Death Valley holds the record for the lowest annual rainfall in the United States — less than 2 inches — and the highest temperature — 134 degrees! It is difficult to imagine plants or animals thriving under conditions like these, but in fact the Mojave Desert is home to many species.

Perhaps the most distinctive plant here is the **Joshua Tree (98).** Actually a kind of yucca, this tree was named after the prophet Joshua. To some early travelers in this region, the extended branches of the tree suggested Joshua's outstretched arms as he pointed in the direction of a promised land. The branches hold clumps of stiff, sharply pointed leaves, dark green in color. Joshua Trees are not found in the lowest elevations of the Mojave, but they are common at middle elevations all around the fringes of this desert.

The fallen branches beneath the Joshua Tree provide an ideal spot for the tiny **Desert Night Lizard (99).** The debris underneath the tree provides a hiding place, insulation against extreme temperatures, and a steady supply of insects to eat. Most lizards are only out during the daytime, but this one is also active at dusk, and in the hottest part of the summer it may roam about at night. The Desert Night Lizard is olive-gray or dark brown with black speckles.

98. Joshua Tree

99. Desert Night Lizard

An insect that can often be found in the springtime among the leaves of the Joshua Tree is the **Yucca-boring Weevil (100).** This all-black beetle has a long curved snout that looks a little like a tiny version of an elephant's trunk. It lays its eggs on the Joshua Tree leaves, and its young (larvae) bore into the leaf buds to feed. Later, the larvae enclose themselves in small cases of plant fiber in the stems. Some scientists think that the slight injury to the tree caused by this beetle is one reason the Joshua Tree develops branches.

Often heard before it is seen, the **Ladder-backed Woodpecker (101)** makes a sharp *pik* call note. It is attracted to the only sizeable tree in sight — the Joshua Tree — where it may excavate a nest cavity in a dying or dead branch. The female lays 4 or 5 white eggs. This woodpecker is recognized by the black and white bars on its back (like the steps on a ladder) and by its black and white face pattern. The male has a red patch on its head.

Along with Creosote Bush (see page 10), **White Bur-sage (102)** covers much of the Mojave Desert. This low-growing shrub has silvery green leaves that help to reflect the intense light of the sun. Horses and burros are very fond of this plant. For this reason it is sometimes called burroweed or burrobrush.

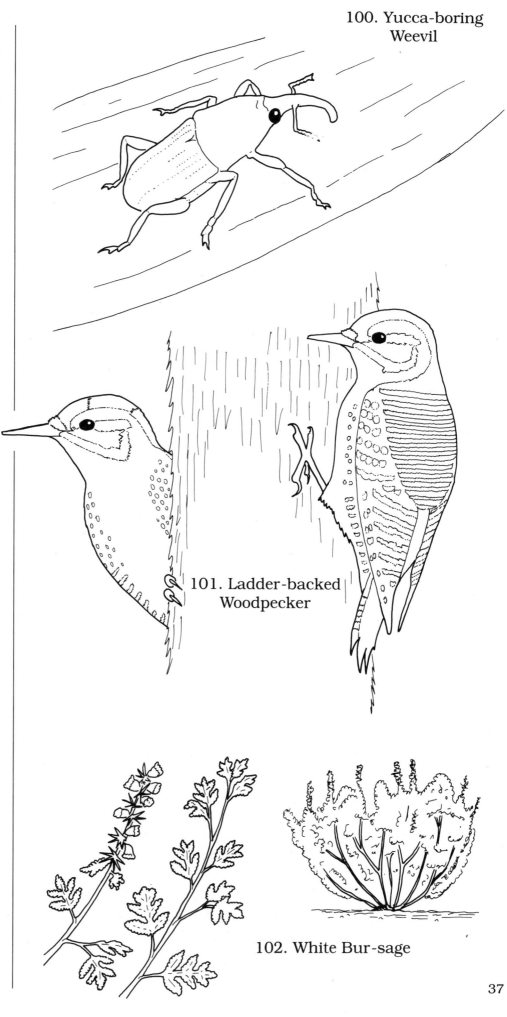

100. Yucca-boring Weevil

101. Ladder-backed Woodpecker

102. White Bur-sage

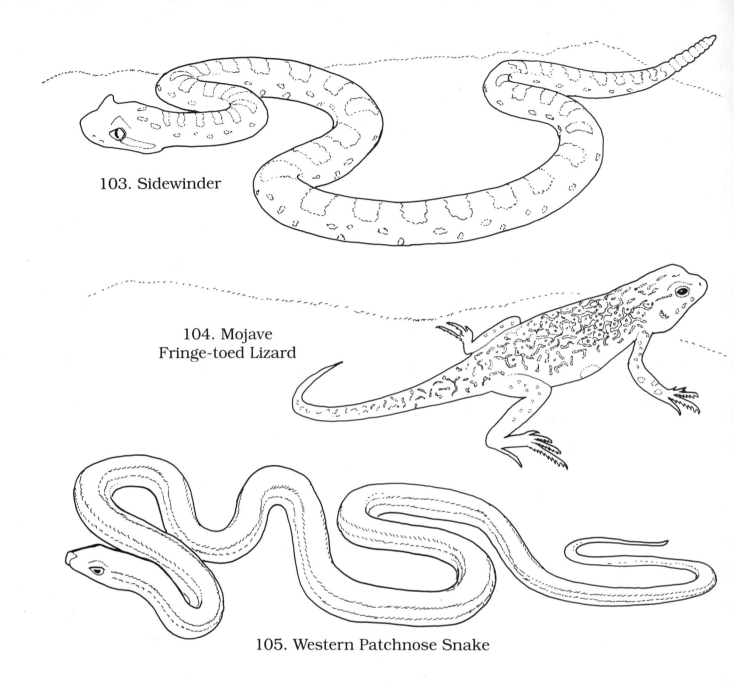

103. Sidewinder

104. Mojave
Fringe-toed Lizard

105. Western Patchnose Snake

When seen in motion, the sand-colored **Sidewinder (103)** is unmistakable. This rattlesnake slithers over the ground sideways, in an S-shaped curve, a method of travel that keeps it from slipping in the sand. It can move with surprising speed in this way, and it is usually found in sandy places, where sidewinding is an advantage. Sidewinders are also called "horned rattlesnakes" because of the special scales above their eyes, which form small pointed bumps that look like horns.

Another reptile that is well adapted to sandy terrain is the **Mojave Fringe-toed Lizard (104).** It has fringelike scales on its hind toes that give it traction so that it doesn't sink when running in the fine sand. The complicated pattern on the back of the Mojave Fringe-toed Lizard provides camouflage among the dunes, and the flaps of skin on its head help to keep sand out of its ear openings. A fringe-toed lizard moving at top speed can stand up on its hind legs and run. If threatened, it can burrow

into the sand so quickly that it seems to simply disappear.

Chiefly active during the day, the fast-moving **Western Patch-nose Snake (105)** feeds on lizards, small mammals, and reptile eggs. This slender-bodied reptile has a wide yellow stripe with dark edges running down the length of its back. It gets its name from the wide triangle-shaped scale that curves back over its snout. The Western Patchnose can be anywhere from 2 to 4 feet long.

A bird that likes desert flats with sparse vegetation is **Le Conte's Thrasher (106).** It is pale sandy colored with dark eyes and a curved bill. It uses its beak as a pick to unearth insects living in the soil. This bird runs on the ground with its tail held above its back and seems to prefer to run rather than fly, unless it is threatened. Le Conte's Thrasher often builds its nest in a saltbush.

A large, weedy-looking shrub that grows in sandy soils is **Four-winged Saltbush (107).** It has light gray-green leaves that help reflect the strong rays of the sun. This bush may grow 3 to 6 feet high. At the end of summer, it produces large numbers of papery bracts shaped like wings. This plant is found throughout our desert regions and is especially common in areas of poor soil where few other plants will grow.

Diamond Cholla (108) is also well adapted to sandy places. This cactus often grows in the form of a very dense shrub. It gets its name from the diamond-shaped pattern on its stems. The Diamond Cholla has very long yellow spines.

Shrews look like small mice with long snouts, but their habits are very different. While mice are mostly seed eaters, shrews are active little carnivores that feed on insects, worms, and other tiny creatures. The grayish brown **Desert Shrew (109)** can often be found among dead vegetation at the base of desert plants. It also sometimes visits woodrat nests. When it is not asleep, it dashes around looking for things to eat, because a shrew may consume its own weight in food every day.

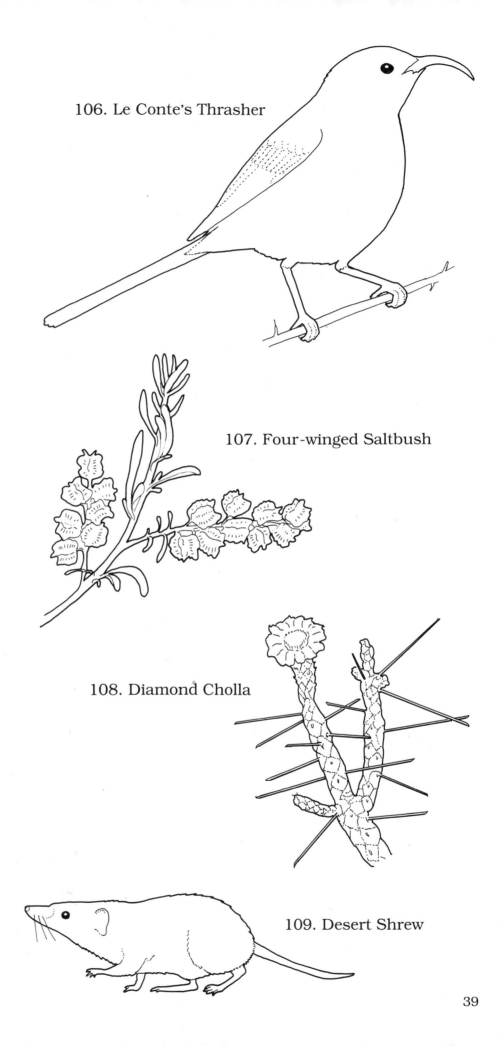

106. Le Conte's Thrasher

107. Four-winged Saltbush

108. Diamond Cholla

109. Desert Shrew

Life Underground

One of the most important ways for animals to escape the heat is to retreat underground. The air is cooler and more humid below the surface of the soil. In some woodrat and kangaroo rat burrows, for example, studies have found that the highest summer temperature reached about 87 degrees Fahrenheit. While this may sound warm to you, it is certainly cooler than the 100+ degree temperatures above ground! Burrowing animals also avoid the drying desert winds that may contribute to dehydration, a loss of water from the body. Finally, underground burrows provide safety from predators. Many desert animals can dig their own burrows. Others take over burrows that are occupied by other animals or move into abandoned burrows.

With its high-domed brown shell, stocky limbs, and short tail, the slow-moving **Desert Tortoise (110)** is easy to recognize. This is the only "turtle" likely to be found far from water in the desert. For up to six months of the year it may sleep in its underground burrow.

When plant growth is at its peak, the tortoise emerges to feast upon leaves, flowers, and cactus pads. The Desert Tortoise has a very long life span; it may live as long as a human.

With strong teeth and long claws on its front feet, the **Valley Pocket Gopher (111)** digs extensive underground runways. It feeds largely on roots and bulbs. If you see a plant suddenly disappear underground, it is probably the work of one of these animals. They come above ground only briefly to gather food.

110. Desert Tortoise

111. Valley Pocket Gopher

112. Long-nosed Snake

Named for its slender, pointed snout, the **Long-nosed Snake (112)** spends the daylight hours underground. This slim reptile has a pattern of red and black bands, with white spots or mottled patches breaking up the black areas.

The **Roundtail Ground Squirrel (113)** also likes to burrow under Creosote Bushes. These small, plain-looking animals scamper around in search of seeds and mesquite pods. They are most active in the mornings and evenings. If threatened, they hug the ground, their sandy tan color blending in with the color of the soil.

During the day you might see a small brown owl with long legs standing on a mound of dirt. This is the **Burrowing Owl (114),** a species that nests in abandoned rodent burrows. If it is disturbed while in its burrow, it may make a rattling noise that sounds like a rattlesnake.

Largest of the kangaroo rats, the **Desert Kangaroo Rat (115)** is buffy colored with a white tip to its tail. It makes its own burrow, often locating the entrance at the base of a Creosote Bush. The strong roots of this plant help prevent the burrow from collapsing. The kangaroo rat is mainly active at night, but it may stay underground on moonlit nights when it can be spotted easily by predators.

The **Harvester Ant (116)** constructs large colonies underground. Each of these ant cities may have more than 20,000 worker ants. You can spot a colony by looking for the round crater of sand around the nest entrance. Queen ants and workers are pale rusty red in color.

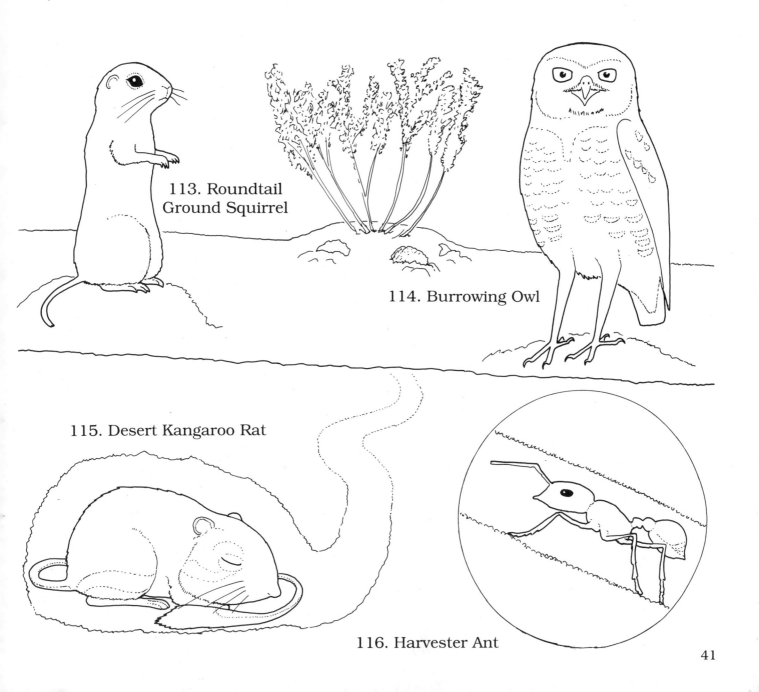

113. Roundtail Ground Squirrel

114. Burrowing Owl

115. Desert Kangaroo Rat

116. Harvester Ant

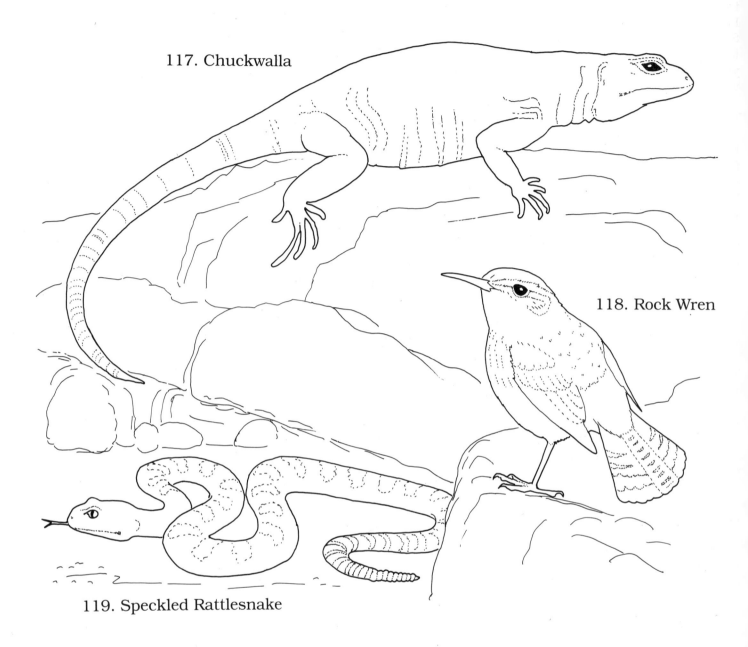

117. Chuckwalla

118. Rock Wren

119. Speckled Rattlesnake

A number of plant and animal species live among rocky outcrops in the Mojave Desert.

A great sunbather, the **Chuckwalla (117)** is a large, flat-bodied lizard often seen lying on top of a rock pile. It likes rocky crevices where it can find shelter and boulders for basking in the sun. One of the largest lizards in the United States, it may be recognized by the loose folds of skin on the neck and sides. Its body color varies from pale yellow to gray. Males have black on the head and forelegs. When disturbed, the Chuckwalla will slip into a rock crevice and then gulp air so that its body swells up, wedging the lizard in place.

The **Rock Wren (118)** is mostly pale brownish gray and is difficult to see among the gray boulders of its surroundings. If your eyes catch some movement, however, it may be the Rock Wren. While searching for insects and spiders to eat, it may pause on a solitary rock and bob up and down several times. A closer look at this bird reveals a buffy tip on its tail and a rusty brown color on its lower back. The entrance to the Rock Wren's nest is often "paved" with little pieces of rock.

At home in the rocky flat-topped hills of the Mojave, the **Speckled Rattlesnake (119)** has a salt-and-pepper pattern that looks a little like weather-beaten granite. This snake is wary and excitable. It will hold its ground when cornered. Like other rattlesnakes, the Speckled Rattlesnake does not lay eggs but gives birth to live young. This snake can be anywhere from 2 to 5 feet long.

With a bald red head like that of a turkey and a large black body, the **Turkey Vulture (120)** is easy to identify. Holding its long wings in a shallow V position, this bird rocks and tilts as it flies. Turkey Vultures perform an important job in nature: they are the cleanup crew, eating the carcasses of dead animals. Vultures have excellent eyesight. Unlike most birds, they also have a keen sense of smell, which helps them find their food.

The **Mojave Yucca (121)** is a plant that favors rocky or gravelly slopes. Some people call this plant "Spanish dagger" because its long yellow-green leaves are shaped like daggers or knives. Fiber from the leaves was used by Native Americans to make ropes and baskets. The Mojave Yucca is another plant that depends on the Pronuba Moth for pollination (see page 12). The stalks of this plant produce whitish flowers that attract the moth.

Another plant that likes gravelly soil is the **Beavertail Cactus (122).** It has flat, blue-green pads that are shaped like the tail of a beaver. This low-spreading cactus grows in clumps 1 to 6 feet wide and produces brilliant rose-colored flowers. Native Americans used the fruit and pads of this cactus for food.

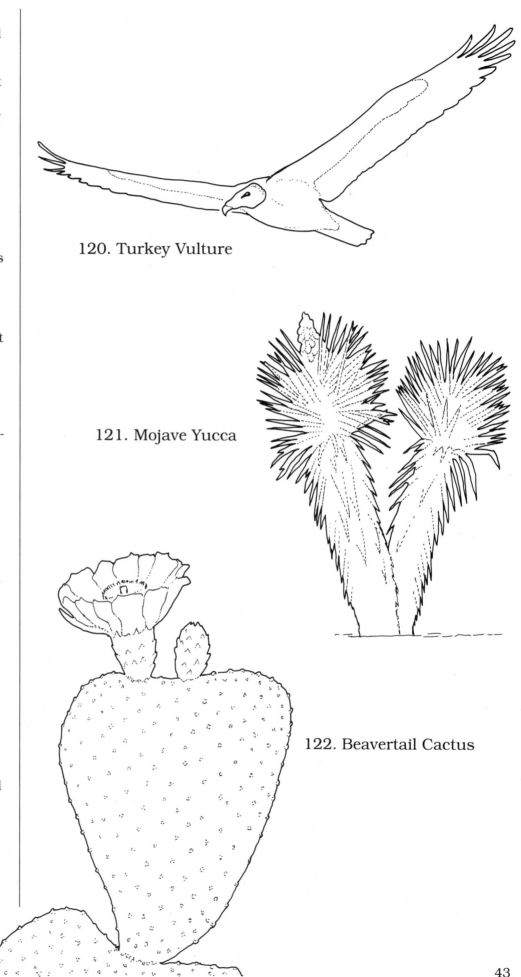

120. Turkey Vulture

121. Mojave Yucca

122. Beavertail Cactus

43

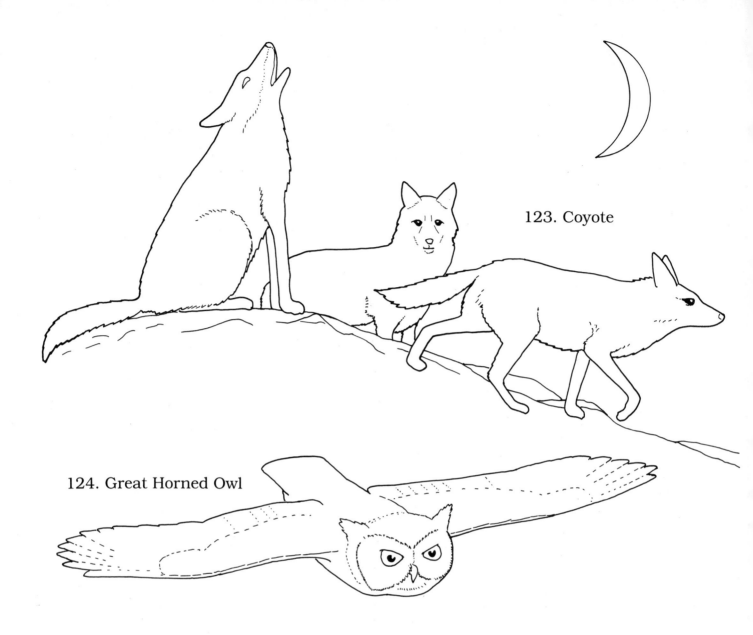

123. Coyote

124. Great Horned Owl

Night in the Mojave Desert

With the setting of the sun, the unrelenting heat of the day begins to ease. Temperatures slowly start to drop, and the humidity increases slightly.

Now the high-pitched howls and yips of the **Coyote (123)** penetrate the dusk. Although you might see this crafty wild dog anytime during the day, it is most active at night. It is reddish gray in color and has a pointed nose. A true scavenger, it will eat almost anything that opportunity sends its way: rabbits, fruit, birds, ground squirrels, berries, insects, or dead animals. The coyote is known as a cunning, intelligent animal because it is very adaptable and manages to survive in many habitats, even at the edges of cities. The coyote is also a good runner, and over a short distance it can put on a burst of speed up to 40 miles per hour.

You may also hear the low-pitched hooting of the **Great Horned Owl (124).** This very large owl lives in many parts of North and South America and is quite at home in the western deserts. It gets its name from the big tufts of feathers that look like horns on its head. A majestic-looking bird, the Great Horned Owl is heavily barred with brown and has a white collar and yellow eyes. It can live in many places, because it will eat practically anything it can catch, including rabbits, frogs, quail, snakes, scorpions, and even skunks.

One of the last nocturnal creatures to come out in the evening, well after dark, is the **Pallid Bat (125).** It has sand-colored fur and very long ears. This bat searches for food on the ground. With its keen hearing, it can detect the slightest sound of a scurrying insect such as a cricket, scorpion, katydid, or beetle.

Dull in color, the **Shield-backed Katydid (126)** looks a little like a stick or piece of wood. Adults have large yellowish bodies mottled with brown or green. This relative of the grasshoppers has very short wings and cannot fly. The male makes a sharp *zip-zip-* *zip* sound, over and over, with long pauses between choruses.

At dusk, the **Desert Banded Gecko (127)** leaves its hiding place under a rock or plant debris. Large eyes and movable eyelids give it an otherworldly appearance. Its light tan body has brown bands. Although most reptiles are silent, geckos communicate with each other by chirping and squeaking.

A relative of the large boa constrictors found in the tropics, the **Rosy Boa (128)** may be seen at dusk, but it is chiefly active during the nighttime hours. It kills its prey — lizards, birds, and rodents — by coiling itself around a creature and squeezing. This snake has smooth, shiny scales. Its body is pale red with three long, brownish red stripes. Full-grown Rosy Boas average 3 feet in length.

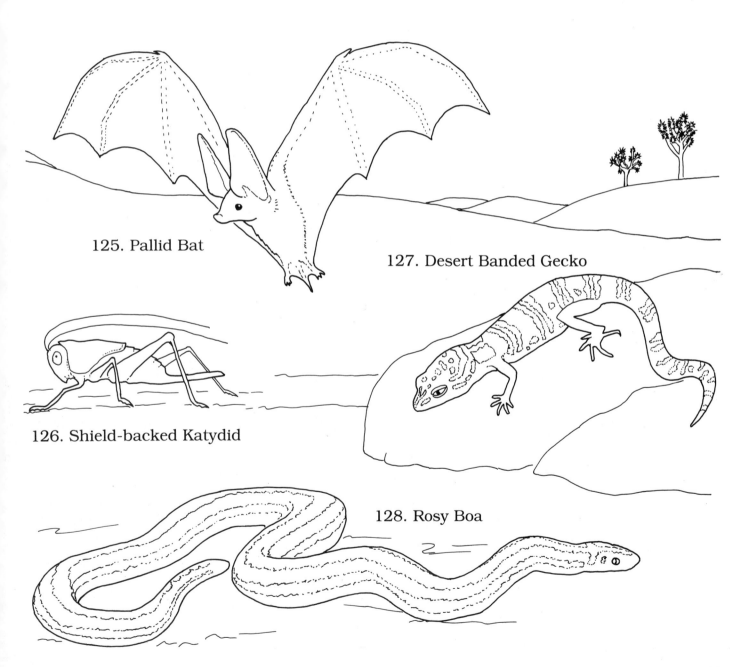

125. Pallid Bat

126. Shield-backed Katydid

127. Desert Banded Gecko

128. Rosy Boa

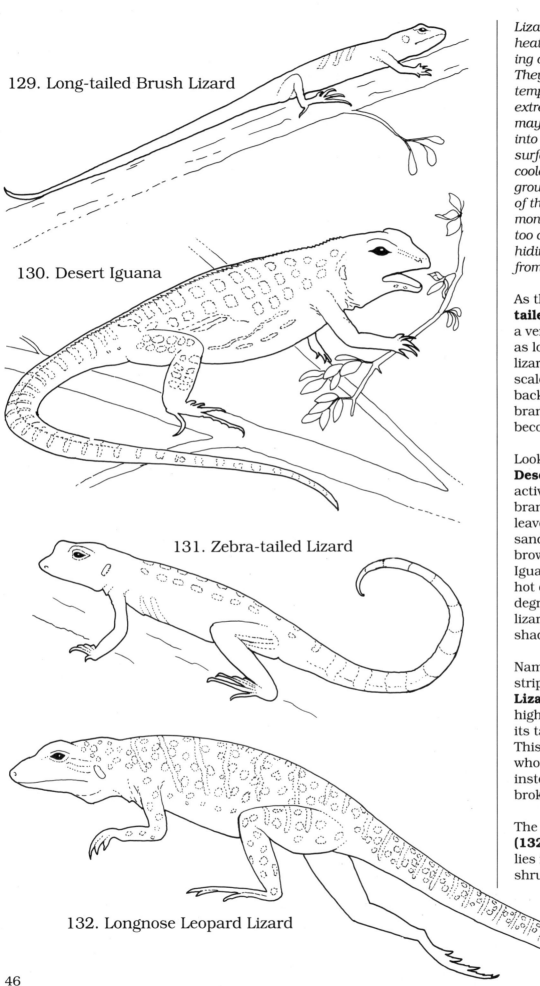

129. Long-tailed Brush Lizard

130. Desert Iguana

131. Zebra-tailed Lizard

132. Longnose Leopard Lizard

Lizards seem to thrive on the heat. You often see them basking on rocks in the sunlight. They do this to keep their body temperatures stable. If it is extremely hot, however, they may wriggle their undersides into the sand just below the surface, where it is slightly cooler, or they may go underground during the hottest parts of the day. During the winter months when temperatures are too cold for them, lizards go into hiding, and seem to disappear from the desert.

As the name implies, the **Long-tailed Brush Lizard (129)** has a very long tail — often twice as long as its body. This gray lizard has a broad band of scales down the middle of its back. It likes to lie along the branch of a bush, where it becomes practically invisible.

Looking almost prehistoric, the **Desert Iguana (130)** is a large, active lizard. It climbs on the branches of plants to eat leaves, buds, and flowers. It is sandy gray in color, with brown patches. The Desert Iguana is often seen on very hot days — up to 115 degrees — when most other lizards have retreated to the shade.

Named for its black and white striped tail, the **Zebra-tailed Lizard (131)** is able to run at high speeds. It curls and wags its tail when it is ready to run. This may distract predators, who then focus on its tail instead of its body. If the tail is broken off, it can grow back.

The **Longnose Leopard Lizard (132)** may be hard to see as it lies in wait for prey beneath a shrub. Its sandy color and leopardlike spots are excellent desert camouflage. This is another species of lizard that likes to run, and sometimes it gets moving so fast that it stands up and runs on its hind feet only.

A bird of open country, the **American Kestrel (133)** is the smallest North American falcon. The male has blue-gray wings with a reddish back and tail. Its striking black and white face pattern is also distinctive. This bird hovers on rapidly beating wings as it gets ready to dive toward its prey. It eats insects and is particularly fond of grasshoppers. When sitting and watching for prey, it often bobs its head up and down.

Fast and elusive, the male **Dragon Lubber (134)** is a challenging target for the kestrel. This grasshopper is mottled brown and gray with very short wings. Unlike the active male, the female of this species is slow-moving and relies on her protective coloration to hide from predators.

Brittlebush (135) provides protection from sun and predators for many desert animals. This low, rounded shrub with gray-green leaves produces daisylike yellow flowers in the spring. Its thick gray stems seem stiff and brittle during dry times of the year.

Catclaw Acacia (136) gets its name from its curved thorns that resemble the claws of a cat. It has compound leaves with small gray-green leaflets. This plant usually grows as a large shrub, though it occasionally grows into a small tree. Pale yellow spiky flowers are followed by twisted seed pods that are a favorite food of quail, doves, and rodents.

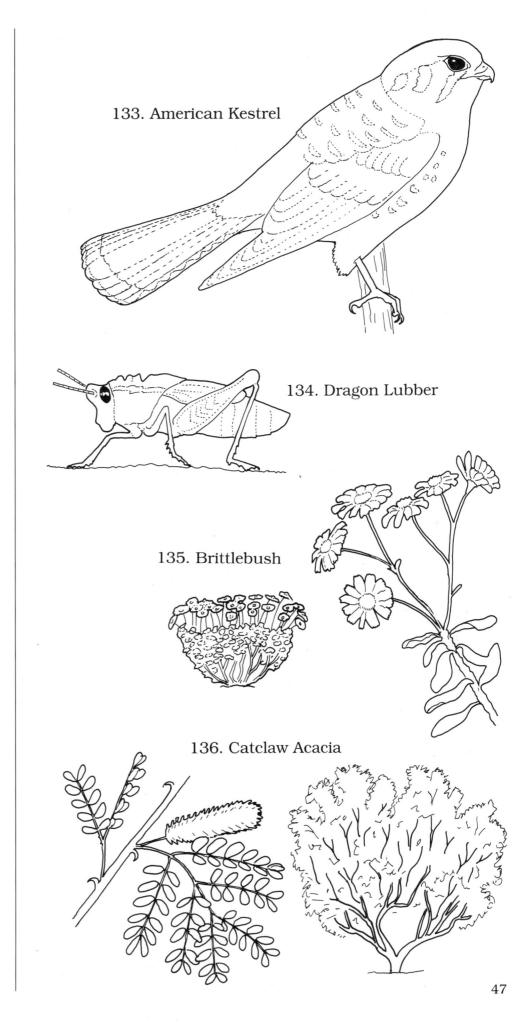

133. American Kestrel

134. Dragon Lubber

135. Brittlebush

136. Catclaw Acacia

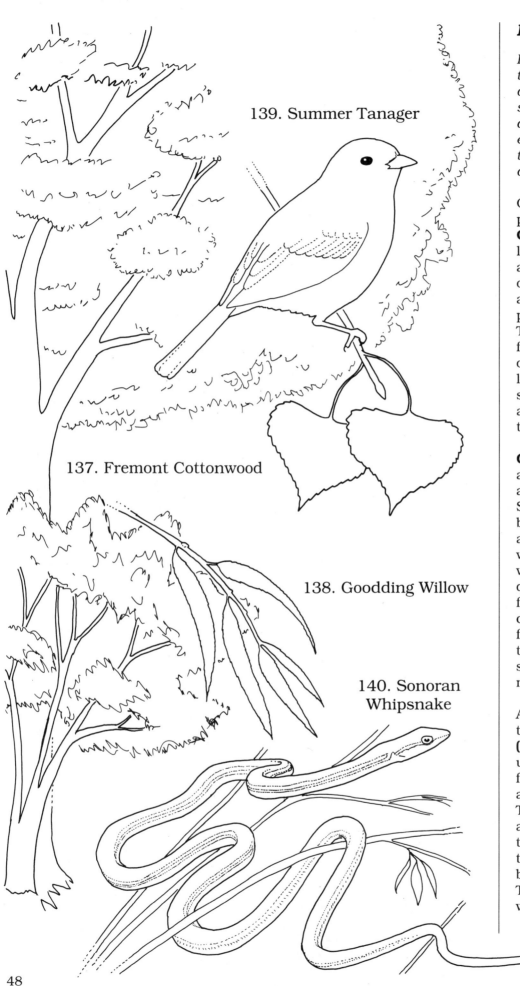

139. Summer Tanager

137. Fremont Cottonwood

138. Goodding Willow

140. Sonoran Whipsnake

Desert Riparian Zones

Riparian areas are the relatively well-watered places along the the banks of rivers, streams, or ponds. In the desert, where water is scarce, even a tiny stream is an important place for both plants and animals.

One of the most distinctive plants here is the **Fremont Cottonwood (137).** These large trees are greedy for water and must have a good supply of it to survive. Cottonwoods are giants compared to other plants found in desert regions. They can grow to be 50 to 75 feet tall with a trunk diameter of over 5 feet. The shiny green leaves of the cottonwood create shade and protection for many animals. In late fall, the leaves turn a brilliant golden yellow.

Goodding Willow (138) is another tree that almost always grows near water. Southwestern rivers that have been left in their natural state are often lined with tall cottonwoods with an understory of willows. Willow stands can be quite thick and provide cover for birds and animals. Like the cottonwood, willows release fluffy seeds into the wind in the spring. The seeds will sprout only if they land on a moist sandbar.

A red bird of riparian zones is the male **Summer Tanager (139).** While the male is almost uniformly rose red in color, the female has yellow underparts and an olive-colored back. These birds are often hidden among the leaves of a tall cottonwood, and you may hear their snappy *pik-i-tuk* call note before you see them. Summer Tanagers feed on insects and will even eat bees and wasps.

The **Sonoran Whipsnake (140)** is a climber and can be found in trees and bushes near water. This slender gray-brown snake has two or three light-colored stripes on each side. A fast-moving reptile that hunts in the daytime, it feeds on young birds and lizards.

The **Gray Hawk (141)** is an uncommon bird of prey that likes to nest in the cotton-woods. This bird is mostly silvery gray, with wide black and white bands on its tail. Listen for its anxious call, a plaintive whistled *cree-er*. The Gray Hawk's nest is a platform of twigs sometimes as high as 70 feet above ground.

Unmistakable with its flaming red color, the male **Vermilion Flycatcher (142)** is particularly fond of the edges of streams. This bird is usually seen perched on an exposed branch near water, flying out to grab insects in the air. During its courtship display, the male hovers high in the air with rapidly beating wings and then slowly flutters back down.

Nocturnal and secretive, the **Gray Fox (143)** sometimes climbs trees at night in search of sleeping birds. It is recognized by its salt-and-pepper coat and long bushy tail with a black stripe down to the tip. The sides of its neck and the backs of its ears, legs, and feet are rusty colored. The Gray Fox preys on small rodents, birds, and insects, and it also eats berries and some fungi.

The water-loving **Sonoran Mud Turtle (144)** may be difficult to spot because it is often covered with algae. For its nest, it digs a hole in a stream-bank. It has an olive-colored domelike shell, and its head and neck are heavily mottled.

141. Gray Hawk

142. Vermilion Flycatcher

143. Gray Fox

144. Sonoran Mud Turtle

145. Saguaro

146. Harris's Hawk

The Sonoran Desert

The Sonoran Desert is home to more species of plants (about 2,500!) and animals than any of the other three North American deserts. Plants here also come in more shapes and sizes, from the spindly Ocotillo to the tall Saguaro. This great variety in plant life means that more kinds of animals can find a home here than in other deserts. The timing of rainfall is what allows for this variety. Gentle rains move in from the Pacific Ocean during the winter months. A second rainy season occurs in middle to late summer, when weather systems from the Gulf of Mexico bring heavy thunderstorms called monsoons.

No plant better symbolizes the Sonoran Desert than the stately **Saguaro (145)** (suh-WAR-oh). This cactus grows very slowly and can take as long as 30 years to reach 2 feet in height. When it is finally full grown, it can stand 50 feet tall and weigh 6 or 7 tons! Only mature Saguaros have "arms". They may live to be over 150 years old. Whenever it rains in the desert, the roots of the Saguaro will soak up all possible moisture and store it inside the body of the plant. The cactus has an accordionlike structure that allows it to expand and contract, swelling up when there is lots of water available. The girth of one of these giants can nearly double in size after a good rain.

In a land with few big trees, the Saguaro is critically important to many other species, especially the birds who nest in its branches or in holes in the cactus. The nest of the **Harris's Hawk (146)** is often cradled in the arms of the cactus. This handsome hawk is dark chocolate brown with patches of chestnut on its wings and thighs. Harris's

50

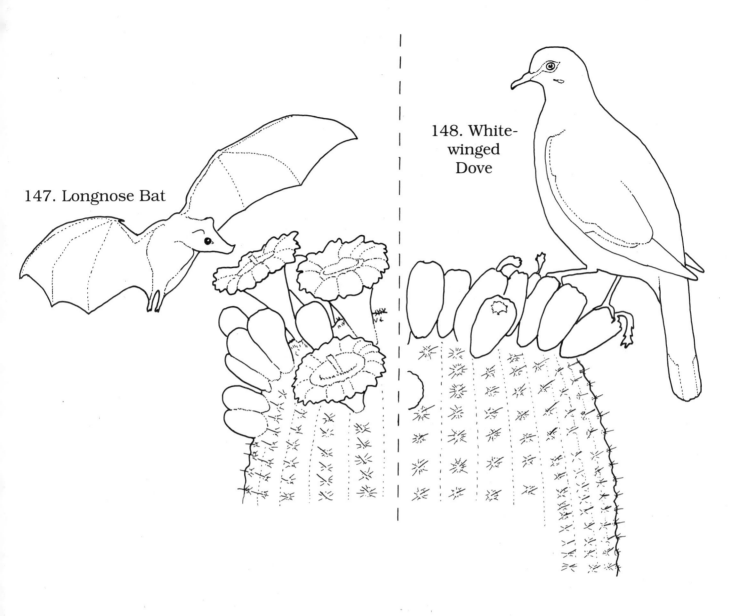

147. Longnose Bat

148. White-winged Dove

Hawks are social birds. They nest in small groups and even hunt as a family.

The Saguaro first blooms when it is about 8 to 10 feet tall. The white flowers open at night and close the next afternoon. The **Longnose Bat (147)** visits these flowers at night to feed on nectar and pollen, helping to spread pollen from one Saguaro to another. In exchange, the flowers provide the bats with protein-rich nectar.

Birds are also attracted to the Saguaro's flowers, and many birds eat the pulpy, red fruit that comes after the flowers. One bird that feeds on both the flowers and the fruits is the **White-winged Dove (148).** This gray-brown bird has white wing patches, white corners to the tail, and bright red eyes surrounded by an area of blue skin. It has a rich, cooing song that sounds like *Who cooks for you?*

The birds knock off some of the Saguaro fruits, which fall to the ground and attract animals like **Yuma Antelope Squirrels (149).** These little squirrels look like chipmunks, with stripes down the sides of their bodies. They eat many different foods, from cactus fruit, seeds, flowers, and leaves to insects. They are active even when it is very hot.

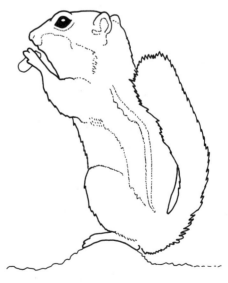

149. Yuma Antelope Squirrel

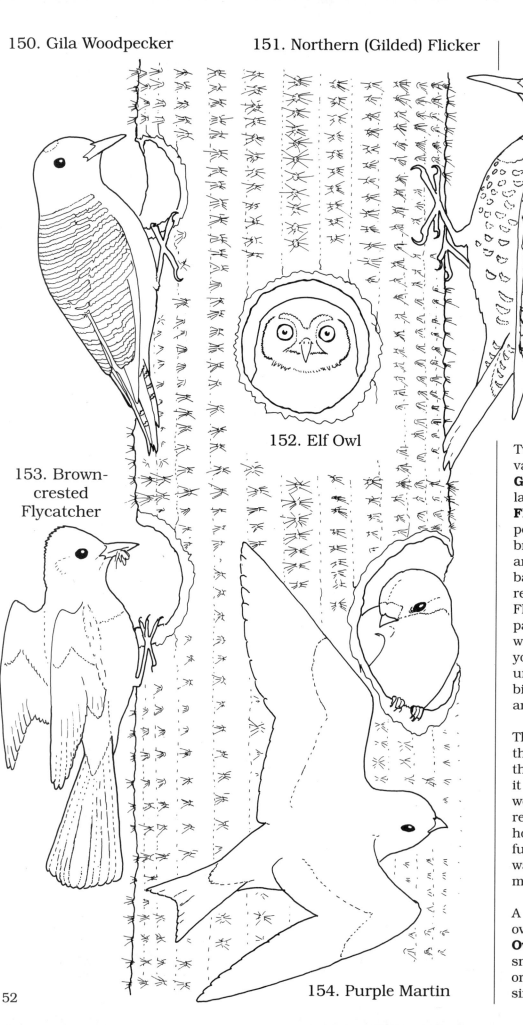

150. Gila Woodpecker

151. Northern (Gilded) Flicker

152. Elf Owl

153. Brown-crested Flycatcher

154. Purple Martin

Saguaros: Apartment Houses in the Desert

Holes in the Saguaro cactus provide nesting places for several kinds of birds. The inside of such a cavity can be as much as 20 degrees cooler than the outside air, and the spiny trunk of the Saguaro gives some protection from predators.

Two woodpeckers often excavate holes in Saguaros: the **Gila Woodpecker (150)** (HEE-lah) and the **Northern (Gilded) Flicker (151).** The Gila Woodpecker is a noisy bird. It has brown underparts and black and white zebra stripes on its back. The male has a spot of red on his head. The Gilded Flicker has a black chest patch, and it has a brown back with dark stripes. When it flies, you can see a flash of yellow underneath its wings. This bird is unusual because it eats ants.

The woodpeckers dig holes in the cactus in which to raise their young. Despite the work it takes to make the holes, the woodpeckers do not seem to reuse them; they make a new hole every year. But these useful nesting sites do not go to waste. After the woodpeckers move out, other birds move in.

A night bird that may use leftover Saguaro cavities is the **Elf Owl (152).** This tiny owl, the smallest in the world, is only 5 or 6 inches tall. The male owl sings from the nest cavity to

155. Whitethroat Woodrat

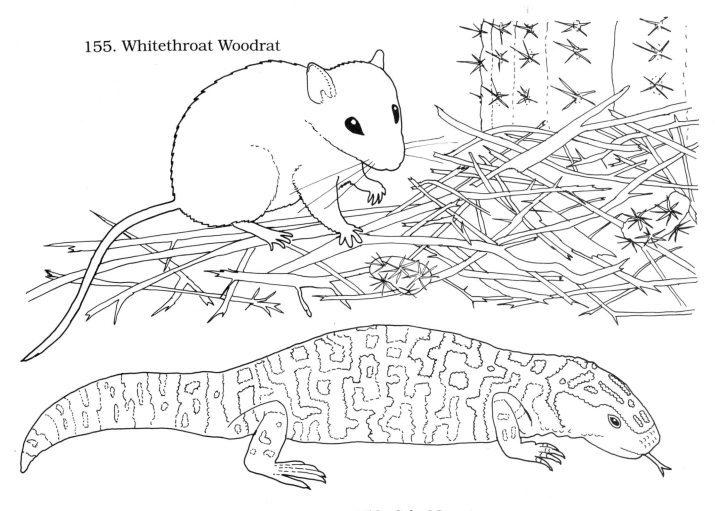

156. Gila Monster

attract a female. Elf Owls eat moths, beetles, and other insects that are active at night. The **Brown-crested Flycatcher (153)** will also nest in old woodpecker holes. This bird is gray-brown above and yellow below, with reddish brown in the wings and tail. It feeds mostly on insects.

Another bird that nests in the Saguaro cavities is the **Purple Martin (154).** This is the largest of the North American swallows. It chases insects high in the air, gracefully circling and gliding as it flies, often with its tail spread. The male is blue-black all over,

with some purple iridescence, while the female is gray and white underneath.

The **Whitethroat Woodrat (155)** may build its nest at the base of the Saguaro. These small mammals are mostly light brown, blending in well against the desert soil. Woodrats are also called packrats because they may fill their nests with any small objects they can find—sticks, rocks, flowers, bits of cactus, pieces of cloth, drinking straws, even wristwatches. Woodrats are active mostly at night. They feed on cactus, mesquite beans, and seeds.

The **Gila Monster (156)** is our only poisonous lizard. It is large and stout, with a bold pattern of black mixed with pink, orange, or yellow. The scales on its back look like beads. The bright colors serve as a warning signal, telling other animals to keep away. Usually slow-moving, it uses its venom to defend itself and is not dangerous unless it is threatened. The Gila Monster spends most of its time underground, under rocks, or in an old woodrat nest. It comes out at dawn or dusk, or on cool spring days. Gila Monsters like to eat bird and reptile eggs and small mammals.

53

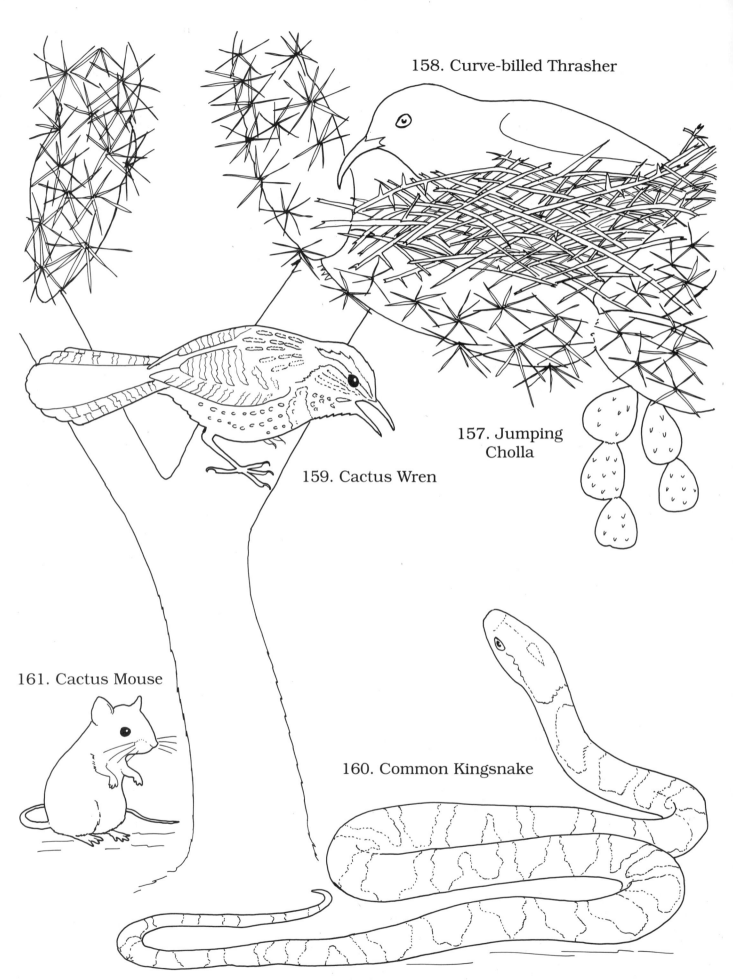

158. Curve-billed Thrasher

157. Jumping Cholla

159. Cactus Wren

161. Cactus Mouse

160. Common Kingsnake

54

The **Jumping Cholla (157)** doesn't really jump, but its joints do break off easily and will stick to an animal (or a person) who barely brushes past this cactus. This is the way this cactus reproduces; it has sterile seeds, so new chollas are "planted" only when joints break off and take root. The sharp spines of the Jumping Cholla protect the plant as well as the desert birds that somehow build their nests among the branches without getting stuck.

A bird that usually chooses cholla for its nesting place is the **Curve-billed Thrasher (158).** It makes a nest of sticks and twigs, and the female lays 3 pale blue eggs. Its *whit wheet* is among the first voices heard in the early morning in the Sonoran Desert. Almost uniformly brown, this bird has yellow-orange eyes and a downward curving bill. This heavy bill is useful for breaking up hard desert soil as the thrasher searches for insects and grubs.

The **Cactus Wren (159)** is another desert bird that favors cholla as a nesting site. It has a conspicuous light eyebrow, heavy black spots on the underparts, and stripes on the back. The Cactus Wren is the largest wren in the United States and is the state bird of Arizona. It makes large, bulky, football-shaped nests and uses these for sleeping as well as for raising young. The Cactus Wren's voice is a monotonous *chug, chug, chug* that sounds a little like a car engine trying to start.

The scolding of Cactus Wrens may be a clue that a snake is nearby. Although the **Common Kingsnake (160)** is not a threat to humans, it likes nothing better to eat than the eggs of nesting wrens and thrashers. This snake has alternating bands of dark brown and pale yellow. Kingsnakes are famous for their ability to eat rattlesnakes. They also feast on lizards, frogs, birds, and small mammals.

If you spot a small, buffy-colored mouse scurrying along the ground, it may be the **Cactus Mouse (161).** These small rodents are most active following seasonal rains when food is plentiful. They often sleep through the hottest and driest part of the summer.

The large hairy spider called the **Tarantula (162)** has a fearsome look, but is actually a gentle creature that tries to avoid humans. Though its venom is not very strong, it should not be handled, since its bite can be painful. These spiders have poor eyesight and rely on a highly developed sense of touch to locate food. They feed on insects, beetles, and grasshoppers. Tarantulas are often seen crossing roads in late summer.

The Tarantula has to watch out for the **Tarantula Wasp (163).** This large, orange-winged wasp uses the Tarantula as food for its young. When the female wasp is ready to lay her egg, she finds a Tarantula and subdues it by stinging it. She then drags the spider to a hole in the ground. She pulls the spider down into the hole, lays a single egg on it, and seals off the entrance to the den. After the egg hatches a few days later, the wasp larva will feed on the host Tarantula for about a month.

162. Tarantula

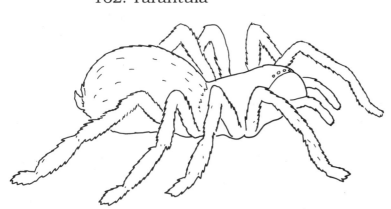

163. Tarantula Wasp

Life in a Desert Wash

In the West, a dry streambed is called a wash. At most times of the year, a desert wash has no water at all. However, after heavy rains it becomes a drainage channel. The dry wash can change quickly into a dangerous waterway, carrying plant, rock, and sand debris, flooding roads and trails in its path.

Like other mesquite trees, the **Screwbean Mesquite (164)** often grows along desert washes, where its roots seek out moisture underground. It is easy to identify when its seed pods are present. The tightly coiled, spiral pods are unmistakable. Mesquite seeds provide an important food for browsing animals.

The male **Northern Cardinal (165)** is easily recognized by the pointed crest on its head and its bright red color, black face mask, and orange-pink bill. But another similarly shaped bird can be found along desert washes. This is the **Pyrrhuloxia (166).** The male is gray and red, but it has a yellow bill. The females of these two species are both buffy brown and are difficult to tell apart. One useful field mark is the stubby yellow bill of the Pyrrhuloxia female, unlike the triangular pink bill of the female Cardinal. Both the Cardinal and Pyrrhuloxia have musical whistled songs that can be heard all along the wash in spring.

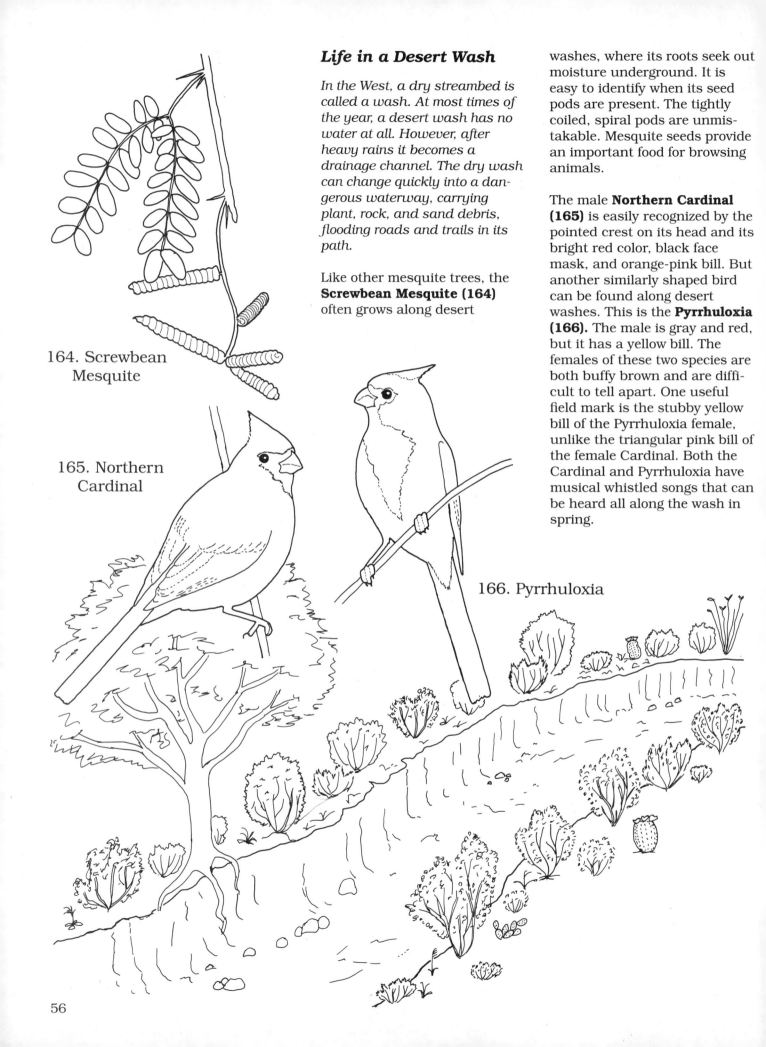

164. Screwbean Mesquite

165. Northern Cardinal

166. Pyrrhuloxia

Only about 2 inches long, the **Red-spotted Toad (167)** is dull olive or gray with small red warts. It likes to live near water, but it can be found in washes where water is present only part of the time. This toad starts to sing during or after rains. Its voice is a high-pitched clear trill.

Desert Hackberry (168) is often found along the edges of washes. This dense green shrub provides excellent cover for quail and other animals that live on the ground. It produces orange berries that attract birds and small mammals.

A medium-sized butterfly closely associated with the hackberry bush is the **Leilia Hackberry Butterfly (169).** Rich red-brown in color, it has two "eyespots" on each forewing. Unlike most butterflies, it seldom comes to flowers; it is more likely to visit dripping sap, rotten fruit, or animal dung. The caterpillars of this butterfly feed on the leaves of the hackberry.

The well-named **Fishhook Barrel Cactus (170)** has long reddish spines that are curved like fishhooks. This cactus is sometimes called "compass plant"

because it has a tendency to lean toward the southwest—the direction of most intense sunlight. In late summer it is topped with flowers that may vary in color from reddish orange to yellow.

Boldly patterned with alternating rings of red and black separated by narrower bands of white or yellow, the **Arizona Coral Snake (171)** is a venomous member of the cobra family. Active mostly at night, it spends the day underground or in rock crevices. It feeds on smaller snakes and lizards. Although it is small and not very aggressive, its poison is extremely dangerous, and the Coral Snake should be avoided.

169. Leilia Hackberry Butterfly

168. Desert Hackberry

167. Red-spotted Toad

170. Fishhook Barrel Cactus

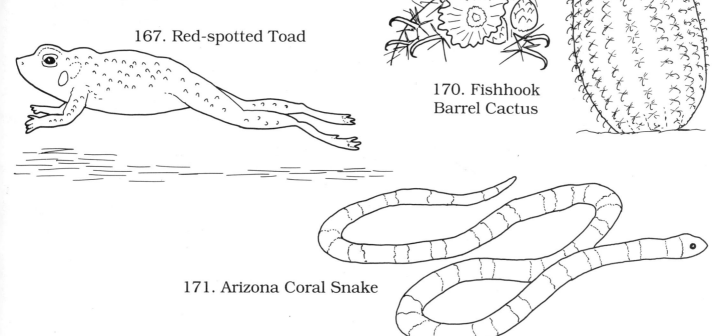

171. Arizona Coral Snake

172. Organpipe

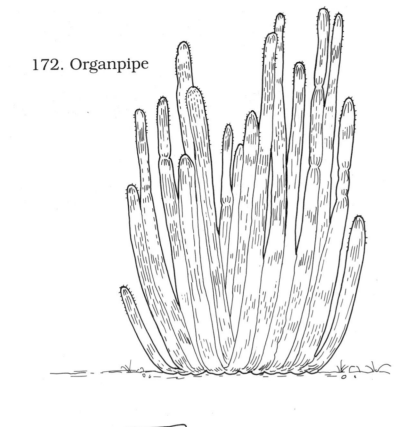

173. Desert Pupfish

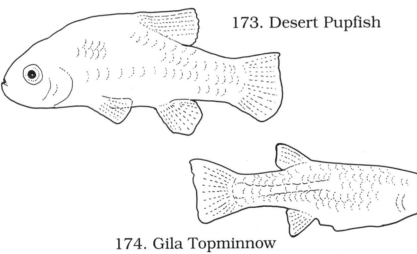

174. Gila Topminnow

175. Colorado River Toad

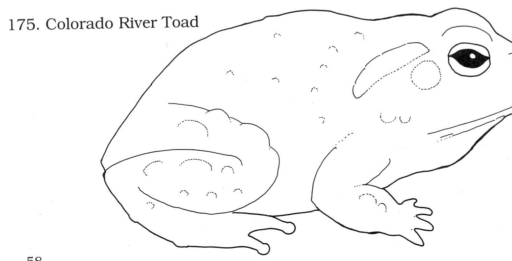

The Saguaro is not the only tall cactus of the Sonoran Desert. The **Organpipe (172)** has many slender branches rising from the base — similar to the pipes of an organ — instead of a tall single trunk. It usually grows to about 10 feet high, but occasionally you may see one that is as tall as 20 feet. The Organpipe has pinkish white flowers that open at night and are pollinated by nectar-feeding bats.

Scattered throughout the desert regions are a precious few small bodies of permanent water, such as ponds fed by natural springs. These water holes provide habitat for several species of small native fish. The **Desert Pupfish (173)** is a true desert fish. The adult males are iridescent blue, while the females are brown. The Desert Pupfish can withstand extreme temperature changes. In addition, it can tolerate the high mineral content of desert watering holes. It eats aquatic plants and tiny aquatic creatures such as mosquito larvae.

Once the most common native fish in the state of Arizona, the **Gila Topminnow (174)** is now endangered. These small fish, no more than 3 inches long, have become rare because introduced (non-native) fish have taken over their habitats. The Gila Topminnow lives in ponds and streams where water is always present. It is the only native fish in Arizona that bears live young.

Heavy-bodied and up to 6 inches long, the dark brown **Colorado River Toad (175)** is the largest toad in the West. Its skin is mostly smooth except for large warts on its hind legs. The Colorado River Toad lays its eggs in long strings — sometimes up to 20 feet long!

During drier times of year, the **Ocotillo (176)** (oh-coh-TEE-yo) may look like an upright bundle of dead sticks. This plant saves water in dry periods by dropping all of its leaves. The plant can grow new leaves quickly after a good rain. The stems of the Ocotillo have a waxy coating that helps seal in moisture. This plant has red-orange flowers at the tips of its branches in spring. Native Americans and ranchers have used Ocotillo branches to make fences. The cut branches will often take root in the ground and grow, becoming "living fences."

Hummingbirds, attracted by the red flowers, often pollinate the Ocotillo. **Costa's Hummingbird (177)** is a species that specializes in living in the desert. It is small even for a hummingbird, only about 3 inches in length. The adult male has a purple throat patch and crown and a green back. In early spring in the desert you might hear his song, a thin, high-pitched whistle.

Named for its conspicuous black and white collar, the **Collared Lizard (178)** needs rocks for basking and open areas for running. The body color of these large-headed lizards varies. Collared Lizards jump from rock to rock and swiftly seize unsuspecting insects or smaller lizards.

With its mottled grayish brown fur and bushy tail, the **Rock Squirrel (179)** is easy to identify. These rodents live mostly on the ground but can also climb shrubs. Rock Squirrels are active during the day and feed on seeds, fruits, and nuts.

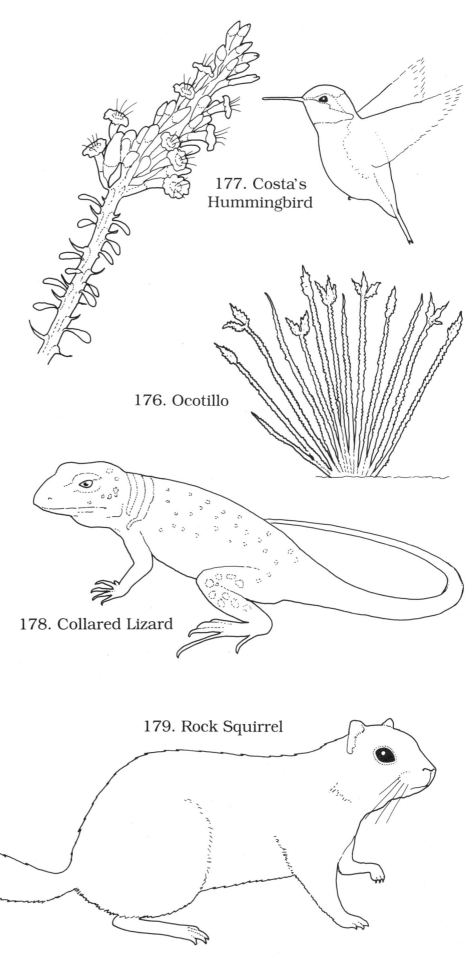

177. Costa's Hummingbird

176. Ocotillo

178. Collared Lizard

179. Rock Squirrel

180. Bobcat

181. Night-blooming Cereus

182. Merriam Kangaroo Rat

Night in the Sonoran Desert

Seen over the wide horizon of the desert, a sunset can be quite spectacular. Although sunset marks the end of the day for some species, for others it is just the beginning.

The **Bobcat (180)** ranges widely at night in search of mice, rabbits, or sleeping birds. It gets its name from its short, bobbed tail. The "wildcat" can be found all over North America. It is quite common in the Sonoran Desert, although you would be very lucky to see one. Tawny brown in color, it has dull brown spots on its body and black spots on its legs and tail. It also has short ear tufts. The Bobcat makes its den in rock crevices or in hollow logs.

The **Night-blooming Cereus (181)** looks like a bunch of dead sticks most of the time. In June, however, it produces spectacular trumpet-shaped white flowers up to 8 inches across that last for only one night.

This plant has a large, fleshy root that accounts for 90 percent of the plant's weight and can grow to 125 pounds. Also called Queen of the Night, the flowers of the cereus fade in the early morning sunlight.

Smallest of our kangaroo rats, the nocturnal **Merriam Kangaroo Rat (182)** is buffy colored with a long tail. This little rodent eats the leaves of winter annuals. In dry years when these plants are scarce, it may not produce any young at all — there would not be enough food for the offspring.

Another distinctive creature of the night is the **Giant Desert Centipede (183),** which can be more than 6 inches long. With its segmented body, it looks a little like a long-legged worm. This kind of centipede has 42 legs, one pair attached to each of its body segments. It likes dark, moist, protected places, and during the day it hides under rocks or pieces of wood. It hunts at night, feeding mostly on insects or small reptiles or mammals. The centipede stuns its prey with a pair of legs equipped with a poison gland.

With large pincers on its front legs and a long tail, the **Desert Hairy Scorpion (184)** is a fearsome-looking creature. It is usually black and pale yellow with dark brown hairs. The Desert Hairy Scorpion spends the daylight hours in burrows or under cover. It comes out at night and lies in wait to ambush insects and spiders. Capturing its prey with the pincers on its front legs, it delivers a paralyzing sting with the stinger located on its tail. This sting is very painful, so if you find a scorpion you should watch it from a distance.

The **Sonoran Shovel-nosed Snake (185)** is active mainly at night. It has a flat, sloping head with a shovel-shaped snout. Its body is yellowish with alternating bands of black and red-orange. This snake can move rapidly through loose sand. It has smooth scales and a streamlined head and body, all adaptations for wriggling through the sand.

For "sand swimming," it's hard to top the **Banded Sand Snake (186).** It is specially adapted for burrowing in the sand; it has smooth scales, its eyes are small and turned upward, and its mouth and nostrils have valves that keep sand grains from entering. The Banded Sand Snake is orange or yellow with black crossbands, and is 7 to 10 inches long. It emerges at night to feed on centipedes, cockroaches, and other insects.

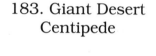

183. Giant Desert Centipede

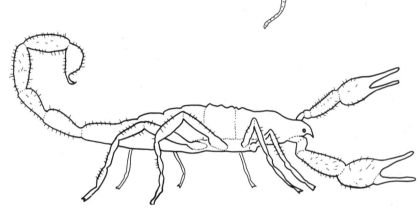

184. Desert Hairy Scorpion

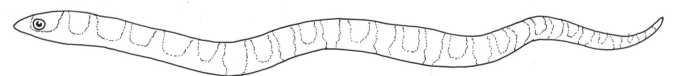

185. Sonoran Shovel-nosed Snake

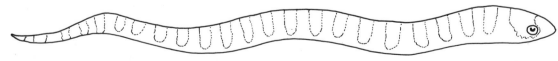

186. Banded Sand Snake

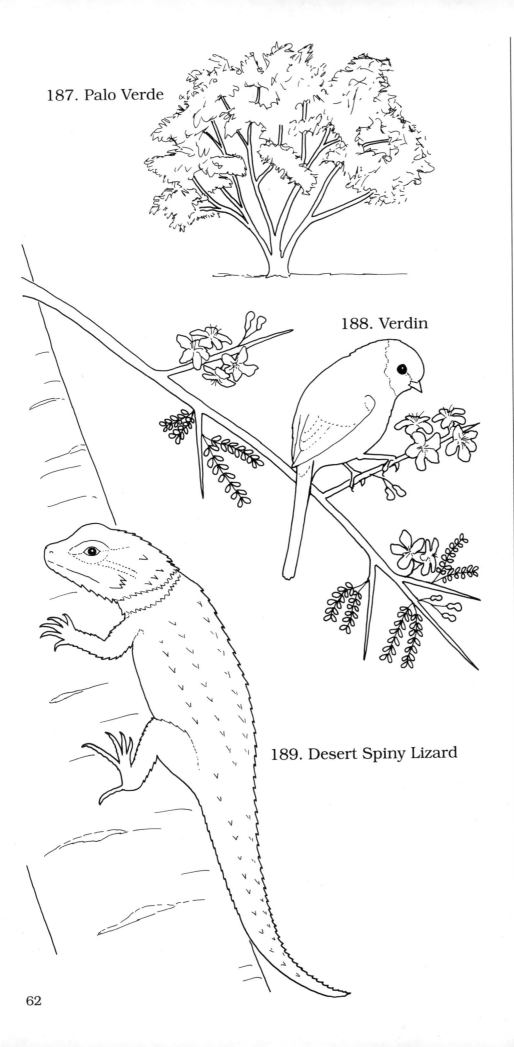

187. Palo Verde

188. Verdin

189. Desert Spiny Lizard

Palo Verde (187) (PAH-low VAIR-day) means "green stick" or "green branch" in Spanish. This is a good name for this tree since its branches and trunk are green. This means that photosynthesis, the process by which plants turn sunlight into energy, may be carried out in its branches and trunk. Most plants carry out photosynthesis only through their green leaves. This tree can continue to draw nourishment from the sun even after it has dropped its leaves, which it does when the weather is too hot or too dry.

The yellow flowers of the Palo Verde attract a number of birds, including the **Verdin (188).** This tiny gray-brown bird has a yellow head. If you look very closely, you may be able to see that it also has a chestnut-colored patch on its shoulder. Verdins feed on nectar in addition to insects, fruit, and seeds. They build nests for sleeping in as well as for raising young. Their large nests are made of thorny twigs.

The **Desert Spiny Lizard (189)** is a fast runner and a fast climber and can often be seen on trees or rocks. This heat-loving reptile is yellowish brown with rough pointed scales. The male has a blue throat and blue patches on the sides of his belly. The Desert Spiny Lizard finds shelter from extreme heat in rock crevices or under logs.

Trees like the Palo Verde provide good daytime cover for nocturnal animals such as the **Collared Peccary (190),** also called the javelina (HAVE-eh-LEE-nah). These piglike mammals have coarse, dark gray hair. They hunt for food in family packs and feed on cactus, mesquite beans, fruit, grubs, and bird eggs. An adult male can weigh as much as 50 pounds. Peccaries will drink

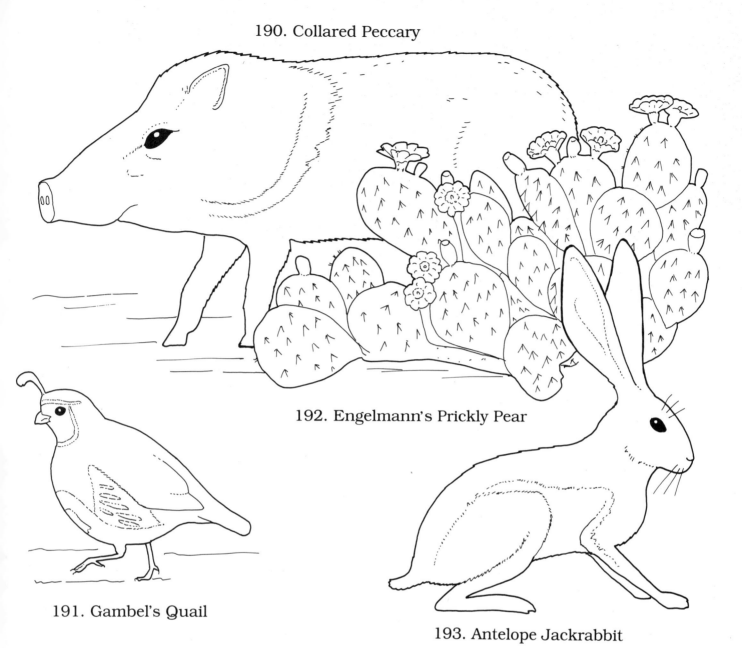

190. Collared Peccary

191. Gambel's Quail

192. Engelmann's Prickly Pear

193. Antelope Jackrabbit

water when it is available, but they can also get moisture from eating fleshy cactus pads.

Gambel's Quail (191) live mainly on the ground. The male of this species is handsome, with his curved head plume, striking black and white face pattern, and rusty red cap and sides. Gambel's Quail travel in large groups during the winter months but then pair off in the spring. The female quail will lay as many as 15 eggs. Upon hatching, the young immediately begin to follow the adult

birds in search of food; they do not spend time in the nest like most other birds. Of the many hatchlings, however, only a few may survive. The large number of eggs makes sure that enough young birds will survive to carry on the species.

Engelmann's Prickly Pear (192) is a cactus with thick, flat gray-green pads that can store water. A number of desert animals get moisture by eating these cactus pads, but to do so they have to avoid the plant's sharp spines. This prickly pear

produces yellow flowers followed by juicy purple-red fruit. The fruit is a favorite food of many desert birds and mammals.

The **Antelope Jackrabbit (193)** is quite a sight with its enormous ears, which are 7 to 8 inches long! This long-legged rabbit is grayish brown on the back but has lighter colored sides. During the day, it usually rests in the shade of a bush. It becomes active in the early evening and feeds until well after sunrise, dining on various desert plants.

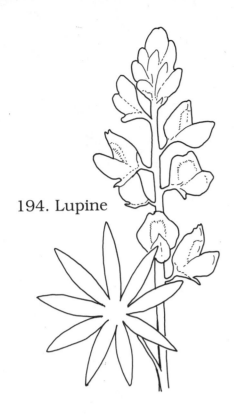

194. Lupine

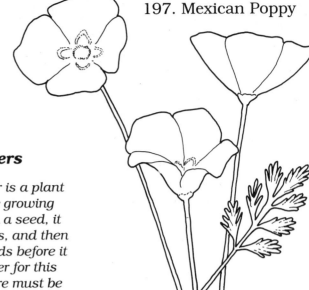

197. Mexican Poppy

Desert Wildflowers

An annual wildflower is a plant that lives for only one growing season. Starting from a seed, it grows quickly, blooms, and then produces its own seeds before it withers away. In order for this life cycle to begin there must be enough rain for the seeds to sprout and enough rain for the seedlings to grow. Here are some colorful desert wildflowers that bloom in the spring.

Lupine (194) has spiky flowers that are violet-blue. **Tidytips (195)** has bright yellow flowers with white tips. **Owl's Clover (196)** is distinctive with its spikes of hot purplish pink flowers. Brilliant golden yellow in color, the flower of the **Mexican Poppy (197)** has four large petals. **Purple Mat (198)** grows low to the ground and has bell-shaped, reddish purple flowers. The flower of the **Desert Chicory (199)** is bright white, tinged with purple underneath.

In a year when there have been good rains during the fall and winter, the desert wildflower spectacle the following spring can be magnificent. The showy arrays of flowering plants attract photographers and wildflower lovers alike. This is yet another spectacular event in the ongoing cycle of desert life.

198. Purple Mat

195. Tidytips

196. Owl's Clover

199. Desert Chicory

133

134

135

136

137

138

139

140

141

142

143

144

145

146

147

148

149

150

151

152

153

154

155

156

157

158

159

160

161

162

163

164

165

166

167

168

169

170

171

172

173

174